BIG ENGLISH PLUS 1

Mario Herrera • Christopher Sol Cruz

PUPIL'S BOOK

Contents

CLIL/Culture	Values	Phonics	I can...
Maths: School possessions notebook, pencil case, pencil sharpener, tablet How many pencils have you got? I've got three pencils. **Around the World: Classrooms**	**Be polite.** Thank you. You're welcome. Please sit down.	**a, t, p, n** an, ant, at tan, tap pan, pant, pat nap	...name classroom objects. ...talk about the things I've got and about rules. ...be polite.
Social Science: Gender baby, best friend, boy, girl, love, man, woman This woman is my mum. This girl is my sister. This is my sister. **Around the World: Families**	**Help your family.** Can I help you? Yes, thank you. Please help me. OK. I can help you.	**i, s, b, d** in, is, it, pin sad, sit bad, bat dad, dip	...talk about my family. ...say how many brothers and sisters I've got. ...ask to help my family.
Science: The senses cake, flower, guitar, hear, ice cream, photo, see, smell, taste, teddy bear, TV I see/taste/hear/smell with my... **Around the World: Flags**	**Keep clean.** Wash with soap. Rinse with water. Dry your hands.	**e, c, g, m** pen, pet cap, cat gas, get, wig map, mat	...name one or more parts of the body. ...talk about my senses. ...say how I keep clean.
Social Science: Weather and clothing cold, desert, dry, hot, jungle, mountains, wet It's cold in the mountains. I'm wearing a jacket. **Around the World: Funny hats** feather, funny, horse race, teacup, watch	**Respect all cultures.** They're wearing traditional clothes from Guatemala.	**o, k, ck** dog, on, pot kid, kit kick, neck, pick, sock	...say what people are wearing and their age. ...talk about clothes. ...respect all cultures.
Art: Shapes circle, flat, houseboat, lighthouse, rectangle, square, yurt **Around the World: Homes** bathroom, bedroom, caravan, caravan site, comfortable, dining room, kitchen, living room	**Help at home.** He's washing the dishes. She's drying the dishes. She's cleaning her room. She's helping her parents.	**u, f, ff** run, sun, up fan, fog, fun off, puff	...talk about home activities. ...name shapes in homes and describe things. ...talk about helping at home.
Social Science: Baby animals calf, chick, kitten, puppy A baby chicken is called a chick. **Around the World: Pets** canary, hamster, mouse, pet, snake	**Be kind to animals.** feeding, walking I'm feeding the chicks.	**r, h, j** red, rock, run hat, hen, hut jam, jet, job	...talk about what animals and baby animals are doing. ...talk about possessions. ...say how to be kind to animals.
Science: Sweet and salty food biscuits, chips, chocolate, crisps, salt, salty, sugar, sweet Crisps are salty. Chocolate is sweet. **Around the World: Special food** birthday, candy, pie, (seaweed) soup	**Eat three meals a day.** I eat breakfast every day. I eat lunch every day. I eat dinner every day. I eat salad for lunch every day.	**l, ll, v, w** leg, let bell, doll, tall van, vet we, web, win	...talk about party food. ...ask and answer about what people have got. ...name sweet and salty food.
Art: Kites bird, butterfly, dragon, fish This kite looks like a fish. It's green. **Around the World: Favourite toys**	**Share your toys.** Sharing is fun! Here's my car. Let's share. Okay. Thank you!	**qu, x, y** quack, quick box, fox, ox, six yell, yes, yum	...name toys. ...say where something is. ...talk about sharing my toys.
Physical Education: Playground games climb, hide and seek, hop, hopscotch, tag Let's play hide and seek. **Around the World: The same game** paper, player, rock, scissors, win	**Look after your body.** Get enough exercise. Get enough sleep. Get enough food and drink.	**ss, z, zz** kiss, mess, miss zap, zip buzz, fizz, jazz	...talk about actions and what I like/don't like. ...talk about games children play. ...say how I look after my body.

Welcome to Class!

1 Listen, look and say.

Listen. Ask and answer.

Hello! What's your name?

I'm Sam. Goodbye!

I'm Anna. What's your name?

Goodbye, Sam!

Listen and point.

1 Hello, pupils. I'm Mrs Smith. I'm your teacher.

Hello, Mrs Smith!

2 How are you, Tim?

I'm fine, thanks.

Look at 3 and role play with your teacher.

Read and match.

1 How are you?

2 What's your name?

3 Hello, I'm Mrs Smith.

a I'm Patrick.

b Hello, Mrs Smith.

c I'm fine, thanks.

Listen, point and repeat.

triangle   circle   square   rectangle   star   heart

 Listen and repeat. Then look at 6. Ask and answer.

 What is it? It's a triangle.

Listen and repeat. Then play a game.

Is it a square?

No.

Is it a heart?

Yes!

8

9 Listen, point and repeat.

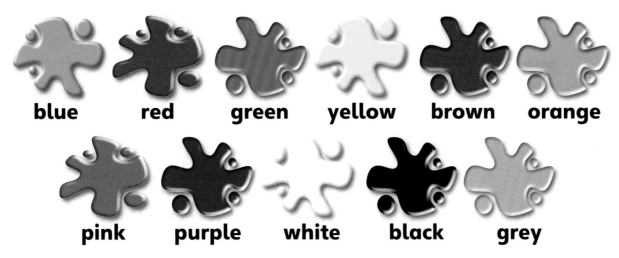

blue   red   green   yellow   brown   orange

pink   purple   white   black   grey

9

10 Listen and circle.

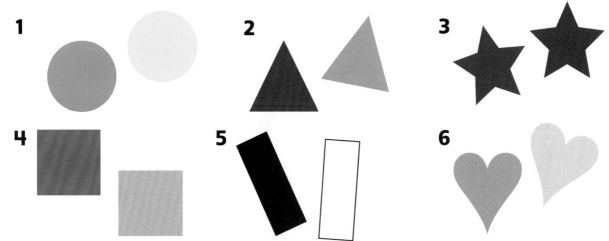

1

2

3

4

5

6

11 Look at 10. Ask and answer.

What colour is it?

It's blue. It's a blue circle.

10

12 Listen and repeat. Then ask the class.

What's your favourite colour?

My favourite colour is green.

Name	Favourite colour

11

13 Listen, point and repeat.

1	2	3	4	5
one	two	three	four	five

6	7	8	9	10
six	seven	eight	nine	ten

11	12	13	14	15
eleven	twelve	thirteen	fourteen	fifteen

12

14 Count the shapes. Then listen and check.

15 Look at 14. Ask and answer.

How many rectangles?

Ten. Ten rectangles.

13

16 Listen and repeat. Then ask the class.

How old are you?

I'm seven.

Name	Age

17 Listen and chant.

Listen to the Teacher!

Stand up!	Point to the window!	Pick up your pencil!
Stand up!	Point to the door!	Pick up your book!
Put up your hand	Clap your hands	Open your book
And turn around!	And sit down!	And close your book!

18 Listen and number.

a

b

c

d

19 Play the game.

Turn around!

Simon says, "Turn around!".

Good Morning, Class!

1 Listen, look and say.

1 desk   2 book   3 crayon   4 rubber

5 marker pen   6 pen   7 pencil   8 ruler

9 chair   10 backpack

2 Listen, find and say.   **3** Play a game.

4 Listen and sing. Then look at 1 and find.

The Classroom Song

Good morning, class.
Good morning to you!
How are you?
I'm fine, thank you.

What is it? It's a rubber.
What is it? It's a ruler.
What is it? It's a pencil.
What is it? It's a crayon.

Now pick up your pen
And open your book.
Say the words
And write with me.
Let's start now. 1, 2, 3!

Chorus

5 Listen and number.

a  b  c  d

6 Look at 5. Ask and answer.

What is it?

It's a chair.

THINK BIG **What is it? Listen, number and say.**
book ☐ backpack ☐ pencil ☐

7 **Listen and read. What colour is the marker pen?**

1

Look, Tim. What is it?

It's a pen.

2

Look! What are they?

They're pencils.

Yes, they're yellow pencils.

3

And what is it?

It's a marker pen. A red marker pen.

Yes! Good, Tim.

4

And what are they?

They're rubbers.

And what colour are they?

8 Look at the story. Then circle.

1 a    b

2 a   b

3 a    b

THINK BIG What happens next? Draw and say.

Language in Action

26

9 Listen. Help Tim and Jane make sentences.

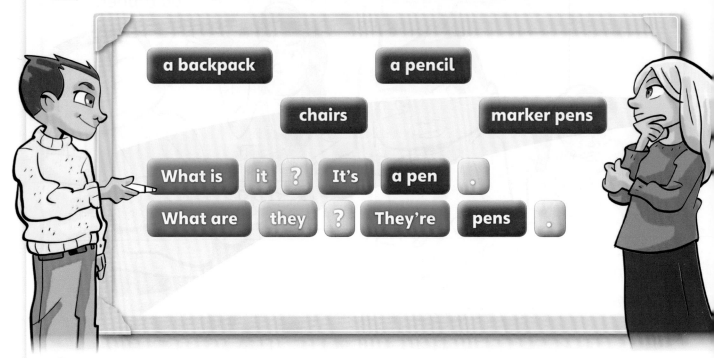

a backpack

a pencil

chairs

marker pens

What is | it | ? | It's | a pen | .

What are | they | ? | They're | pens | .

10 Circle and colour. Then circle and draw.

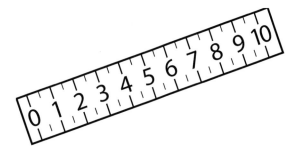

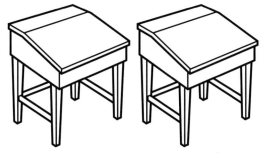

1 What is it? / What are they?
They're rulers. / It's a ruler.
It's blue. / They're blue.

2 What are they? / What is it?
It's a desk. / They're desks.
It's red. / They're red.

3 What is it? / What are they?
They're books. / It's a book.
It's yellow. / They're yellow.

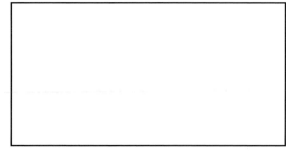

4 What is it? / What are they?
They're rubbers. / It's a rubber.
It's brown. / They're brown.

28

 Listen and stick. Then say.

1

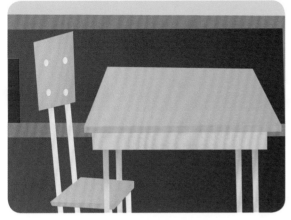

2

3

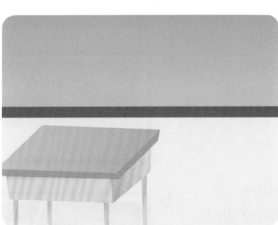

4

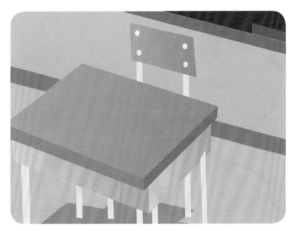

12 **Look at 11. Ask and answer.**

What is it?

What are they?

It's...

They're...

13 **Draw and say.**

14 **Look, listen and repeat. Then say.**

1 pencil case   **2 tablet**   **3 pencil sharpener**   **4 notebook**

I've got a...

15 **Look, listen and read. Then match.**

Luke

1 I've got a tablet, three notebooks and a green pencil sharpener.

a

Emma

2 I've got a yellow notebook and a pink pencil sharpener. My pencil case is blue.

b

Ahmed

3 I've got two notebooks and a tablet. My pencil case is purple.

c

THINK BIG **How many...? Say.**

16 **Look at 15. Count and write.**

	pencil sharpener	notebook	pen
Luke			
Emma			
Ahmed			

17 **Do a class survey.**

	Me		
pencils			
notebooks			
rubbers			

How many pencils have you got?

I've got seven pencils.

PROJECT

18 **Make a My Pencil Case poster. Then present it to the class.**

My pencil case is blue. I've got...

My Pencil Case

32

19 Look, listen and repeat.

1

Stand up!

2

Sit down!

3

Look!

4

Don't talk!

5

Don't run!

6

Don't eat!

Stand up!	Don't talk!
Sit down!	Don't run!
Look!	Don't eat!

20 Look, read and match.

1

a Put up your hand!

2

b Sit down!

3

c Don't clap your hands!

4

d Don't close your book!

21 Read and circle.

School Rules

1 **Talk / Don't talk** in class.   ✗
2 **Listen / Don't listen** to your teacher.   ✔
3 **Look / Don't look** at the board.   ✔
4 **Eat / Don't eat** in class.   ✗
5 **Run / Don't run** in class.   ✗
6 **Do / Don't do** your homework.   ✔

22 Play the game.

Simon says,
"Cross your arms!"

Don't cross
your arms!

23 Draw two home rules.

✗

✔

24 Look, listen and repeat.

1 Africa

2 The United States of America

3 China

25 Listen and read. Then match.

1

In the United States of America, I've got a big classroom. My desk is small and my chair is small, too. I've got a pencil case and I've got marker pens, pencils and crayons. I've got a rubber and a ruler, too.

a

2

My classroom in China is big. My desk is big, too. I've got a pen and a notebook. I've got a tablet and a green pencil sharpener.

b

3

This is my classroom in Africa. It's small. I've got a small desk. I've got a black backpack and a yellow pencil. I've got notebooks, too.

c

26 **Look at 25. Read and ✔.**

	Africa	China	U.S.A.
black backpack			
tablet			
big desk			
small desk			
big classroom			
notebook			
yellow pencil			

27 **What have you got on your desk? Draw and say.**

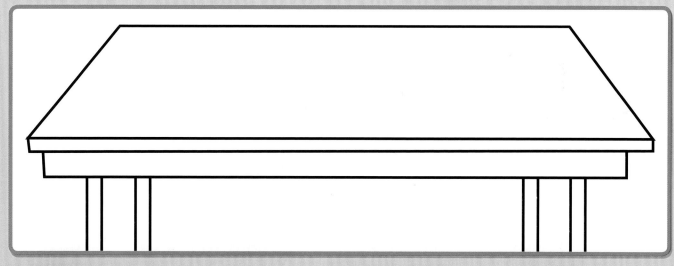

It's a… . They're… .

TH NK BIG **What can you find in classrooms everywhere?**

36
28 Listen and find the picture. Then listen and repeat.

a

b

29 Look and number. Then say.

Thank you. ☐

Please sit down, Anna. ☐

Thank you, Susie. ☐

You're welcome. ☐

THINK BIG How can you be polite in class?

30 **Listen, look and repeat.**

1 a   **2** t   **3** p   **4** n

 31 **Listen and find. Then say.**

pan   **ant**   **nap**   **tap**

 32 **Listen and blend the sounds.**

1 a-n   an   **2** p-a-t   pat

3 p-a-n-t   pant   **4** t-a-n   tan

5 a-t   at

33 **Underline a, t, p and n. Then listen and chant.**

Pat the ant
Has got a tan.
Pat the ant
Takes a nap.

34 **Look and find the differences. Then listen and check.**

Picture A

Picture B

35 **Listen and play a game.**

44
36 Listen and circle.

1

2

3

37 Read and match.

1 Don't run!

2 Sit down!

3 Please don't talk!

4 Eat, please!

a

b

c

d

I Can

- [ ] name classroom objects.
- [ ] talk about the things I've got and about rules.
- [ ] be polite.

My Family

45

1 Listen, look and say.

1 grandad
2 grandma
3 mum
4 dad
5 brother
6 sister
7 me
8 parents (mum and dad)
9 grandparents (grandma and grandad)

46

2 Listen, find and say.   **3** Play a game.

4 Listen and sing. Then look at 1 and find.

My Family

My family, my family!
This is my family.
He's my brother
And she's my sister.

My dad, my mum!
My sister, my brother!
We have so much fun!
I love them.

My family, my family.
I love my family!
I love them
And they love me.
I love my family!

5 Look at 4 and circle the correct answer.

1 grandad / dad   2 grandma / sister
3 mum / brother   4 sister / brother

6 Look at 4. Ask and answer.

Who's he?

He's my grandad.

**THINK BIG Are all families the same?
Who's in your family?**

song/vocabulary Unit 2 **27**

50

7 **Listen and read. How many brothers? How many sisters?**

A Big Family

1. Is this your photo album, Tim?

   Yes, this is my family.

2. Who are they?

   They're my parents.

3. How many brothers and sisters have you got?

   I've got one brother and one sister.

4. Who's she?

   She's my sister.

   Oh, she's Jane!

8 Look at the story. Then circle.

1 She's my mum. a b

2 He's my dad. a b

3 They're my brother and sister. a b

THINK BIG Who's missing? Draw.

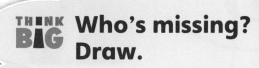

51

9 Listen. Help Tim and Jane make sentences.

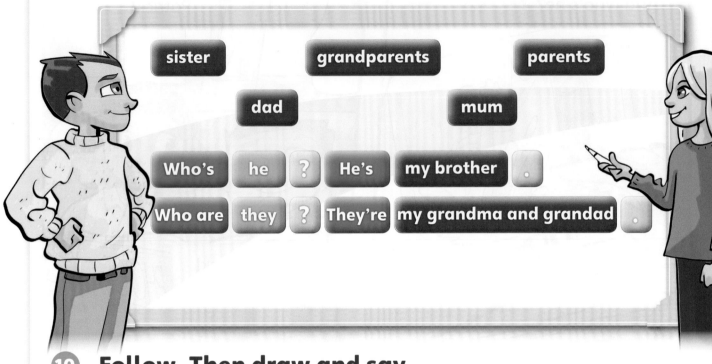

sister   grandparents   parents

dad   mum

Who's | he | ? | He's | my brother | .

Who are | they | ? | They're | my grandma and grandad | .

10 Follow. Then draw and say.

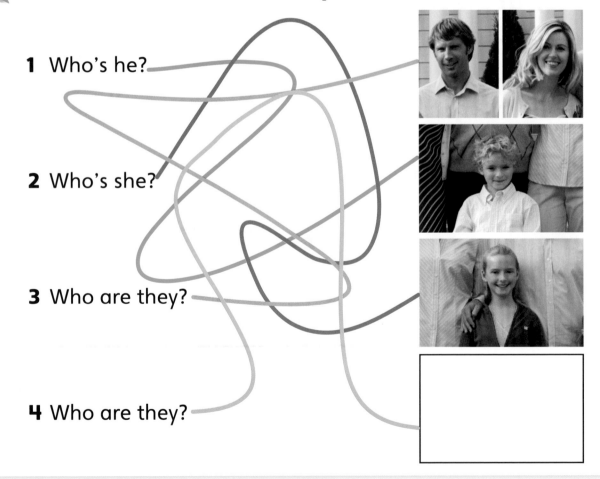

1 Who's he?

2 Who's she?

3 Who are they?

4 Who are they?

53

11 **Listen and stick. Then say.**

1

2

3

4

12 **Look at 11. Role play with a partner.**

How many brothers and sisters have you got?

I've got two sisters.

You're number...

13 **Draw and say.**

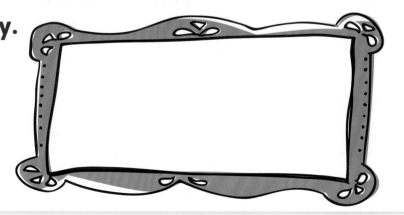

14 **Look, listen and repeat. Then say.**

1 boy   **2 girl**   **3 man**   **4 woman**

> This is a boy. He's my brother.

 15 **Listen, read and point. Is the baby a boy or a girl?**

This is a picture of my family. Look at the boys. They're my brothers. The girl is my friend. She's my best friend. Her name's Mia. This man is my dad. This is my mum and the baby is my baby sister! Her name's Anna. This woman is my grandma. I love my family!

 **Is your teacher a man or a woman?
Is your best friend a boy or a girl?**

16 Look at 15. Circle T for true and F for false.

1 I've got one brother.   T   F

2 The girl is my best friend.   T   F

3 My dad is a boy.   T   F

4 I've got a baby sister.   T   F

5 Anna is a woman.   T   F

6 Mia is my best friend.   T   F

17 Draw your family. Then ask and answer.

Who's this?

This is my brother.

PROJECT

18 Make a Family poster. Then present it to the class.

My Family

This man is my dad and this woman is my mum.

19 **Look, listen and repeat.**

This is my photo album. These are my family pictures.

1 These are my parents. This is my dad and this is my mum.

2 These are my grandparents. This is my grandad and this is my grandma.

3 This is my sister, Sandra. This is me. My name's Mike.

4 These are my brothers. I've got three! This is Andy, this is Sam and this is Jason.

🧍	🧍🧍
This is my dad.	These are my parents.
This is my mum.	These are my grandparents.
This is my sister.	These are my brothers.

20 **Read and match.**

1 my sisters.

3 my brother.

5 my mum.

This is
These are

2 my grandad.

4 my parents.

6 my grandparents.

21 **Read and find.**

This is my family. Look at my grandma. Her name's Anne. This is my grandad. His name's Bob.

The woman is my mum. Her name's Emma. This is my dad. His name's Joe.

I've got a brother and a sister. His name's Pete and her name's Megan.

This is me. My name's Amy.

This is me.	My name's Amy.
This is my brother.	His name's Pete.
This is my sister.	Her name's Megan.

22 **Read and circle.**

1 This is my brother. **Her** / **His** name's Thomas.

2 This is my mum. **Her** / **My** name's Penny.

3 This is my baby sister. **My** / **Her** name's Leyla.

4 This is my grandma. **My** / **Her** name's Betty.

5 This is my sister. **His** / **Her** name's Katie.

6 This is my dad. **His** / **My** name's Batu.

grammar (*This is my dad. These are my brothers.*) Unit 2 **35**

23 **Look, listen and repeat. Then say.**

Family and Friends

1

Maria

2

Minjoon

3

Celine

Who's she? She's Maria. She's from Mexico.

24 **Listen and read. Then write the names.**

¹ Maria is a girl. She's my friend. She's my best friend. She's from Mexico.

² Minjoon is my friend, too. He's a boy. He's seven. He's from South Korea.

³ My sister is ten. I love my sister. Her name's Celine. She's from France. I'm from France, too!

⁴ I love my family and I love my friends, too.

Family	Friends

25 **Look at 24. Read and circle.**

1 Minjoon is a **boy** / **girl**.

2 Maria is my **friend** / **best friend**.

3 My sister's name is **Maria** / **Celine**.

4 Minjoon and Maria are my **family** / **friends**.

5 Celine is my **best friend** / **sister**.

26 **Read, circle and write. Then draw.**

My best friend is a **boy** / **girl**. **His** / **Her** name is _____.

This is my **brother** / **sister** / **mum** / **dad**. **His** / **Her** name is _____.

How many friends have you got?
Have you got a best friend?
What's his/her name?

62

 27 **Listen and read. Then circle.**

1 Pam helps her **brother** / **sister**.

2 Tommy helps his **brother** / **sister**.

28 **Can you help? Role play with a partner.**

THINK BIG **Can you help your family?**
Can you help more?

64

29 **Listen, look and repeat.**

1 i   **2** s   **3** b   **4** d

65

30 **Listen and find. Then say.**

sit   in   dad   bat

66

31 **Listen and blend the sounds.**

1 i-s   is   **2** p-i-n   pin   **3** b-a-d   bad

4 d-i-p   dip   **5** s-a-d   sad   **6** i-t   it

67

32 **Underline i, s, b and d. Then listen and chant.**

Don't sit, sit, sit
On a pin, pin, pin.
It's bad, bad, bad
To sit on a pin!

33 Work with a partner. Ask and answer. Then draw.

34 Play a game.

69
35 Listen and ✔.

1 a  **b**  **2 a**  **b**

3 a  **b**  **4 a**  **b**

70
36 Listen and number.

a  **b**  **c**

I Can
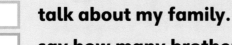
☐ talk about my family.
☐ say how many brothers and sisters I've got.
☐ ask to help my family.

unit 3 My Body

1 Listen, look and say.

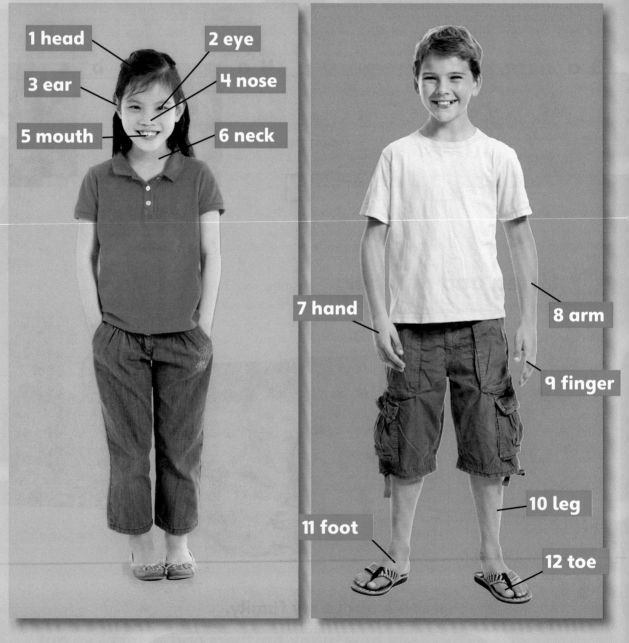

1 head
2 eye
3 ear
4 nose
5 mouth
6 neck
7 hand
8 arm
9 finger
10 leg
11 foot
12 toe

2 Listen, find and say.   **3** Play a game.

Listen and sing. Then look at 1 and find.

My Body Song

Have you got two ears?
Have you got one mouth?
Have you got two eyes?
Yes, I have. Yes, I have.

I've got ten fingers.
I've got ten toes.
I've got two feet
And one big nose!

And have you got long legs?
And have you got short hair?
And have you got small hands?
I sing my body song, my body song,
I sing my body song again!

75

5 Listen and ✓.

1 a    b

2 a   b

3 a 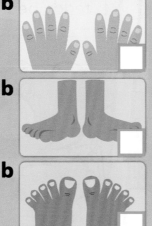   b

6 Look at 5. Ask and answer.

How many ears have you got?

I've got two ears.

THINK BIG Have you got short or long hair? Who do you know who's got short or long hair?

77
7

Listen and read. What's the teddy bear's name?

8 Look at the story. Circle Bobo.

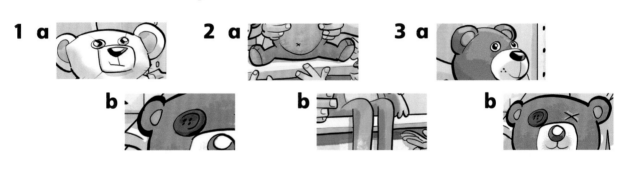

THINK BIG What's your favourite toy? What does it look like? Draw and say.

78

9 Listen. Help Tim and Jane make sentences.

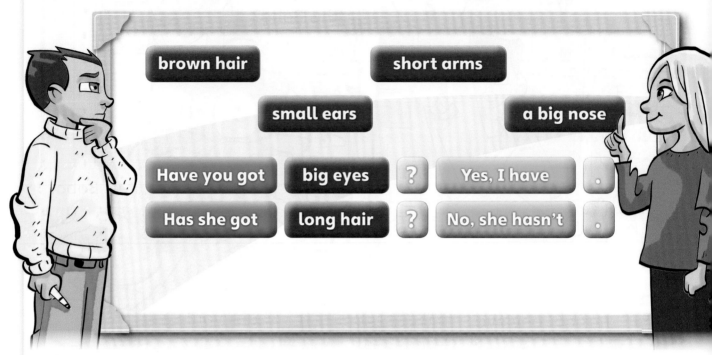

| brown hair | | short arms |
| small ears | | a big nose |

| Have you got | big eyes | ? | Yes, I have | . |
| Has she got | long hair | ? | No, she hasn't | . |

10 Read and circle. Draw and say.

1 Has she got short hair?
Yes, she has. / No, she hasn't.

2 Has he got long legs?
Yes, he has. / No, he hasn't.

3 Has it got small ears?
Yes, it has. / No, it hasn't.

4 Has your grandad got white hair?
Yes, he has. / No, he hasn't.

80
11 **Listen and stick. Then say.**

1

2

3

4

12 **Look at 11. Ask and answer.**

I've got a long neck.

Have you got long arms?

No, I haven't.

Are you number...?

13 **Draw and say.**

81
14 Look, listen and repeat.

1 see   **2 smell**   **3 taste**   **4 hear**

82
15 Look, listen and read. Then match. What do you taste with?

1 I've got two eyes. I see with my eyes. Look! I see a photo.

2 I've got one nose. I smell with my nose. I smell a flower.

3 I've got one mouth. I taste with my mouth. Mmm! I taste cake!

4 I've got two ears. I hear with my ears. Listen! I hear a guitar.

a

photo

b

cake

c

guitar

d

flower

THINK BIG Can you see, hear, taste or smell these things?

16 **Look at 15. Circle T for true and F for false. Correct the false sentences.**

1 I taste ice cream with my nose. **T** **F**
2 I see photos with my eyes. **T** **F**
3 I taste cake with my ears. **T** **F**
4 I hear a guitar with my ears. **T** **F**
5 I smell flowers with my eyes. **T** **F**
6 I see a toy with my eyes. **T** **F**

I taste ice cream with my mouth.

17 **Draw and say.**

1 I see

2 I smell

cake   flower   guitar
ice cream   photo   song
star   teddy bear   TV

3 I taste

I see with my eyes. I see a star.

4 I hear

PROJECT

18 **Make a My Senses poster. Then present it to the class.**

I taste pizza.

My Senses

I hear...   I see...   I taste...   I smell...

84

19 Look, listen and repeat.

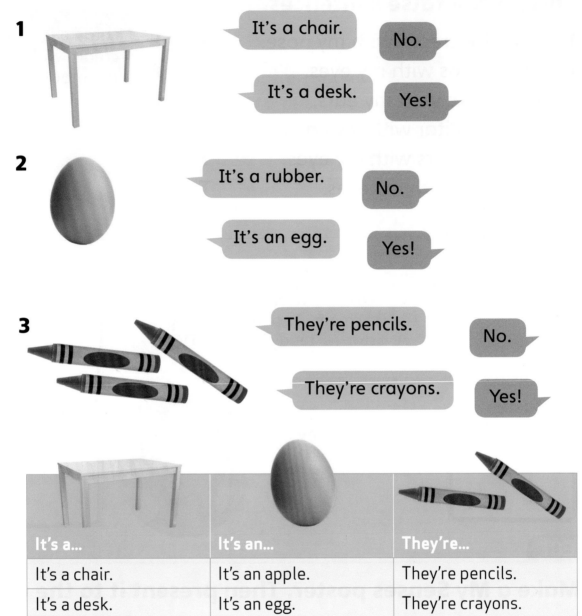

1 It's a chair. No.

It's a desk. Yes!

2 It's a rubber. No.

It's an egg. Yes!

3 They're pencils. No.

They're crayons. Yes!

It's a...	It's an...	They're...
It's a chair.	It's an apple.	They're pencils.
It's a desk.	It's an egg.	They're crayons.

20 Read and circle.

1 **It's a / It's an** apple.

2 **It's a / They're** rectangles.

3 **It's a / It's an** circle.

4 **It's a / It's an** orange.

5 **It's a / They're** notebooks.

6 **It's a / They're** foot.

21 **Look and read. Put a ✔ or a ✗ in the box.**

1 They're hands. ☐

2 They're toes. ☐

3 It's a finger. ☐

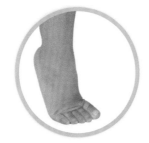

4 It's a foot. ☐

22 **Read and match.**

apple.   balls.   **It's a**   marker pens.   orange.

box.   chairs.   pens.   square.

            egg.   **It's an**   rubber.

circle.   triangle.

        insect.   **They're**   ear.

23 **Look around your classroom. Point and say with a partner.**

They're desks.

It's a computer.

24 **Look and say. What other colours do you know?**

Flags of All Colours

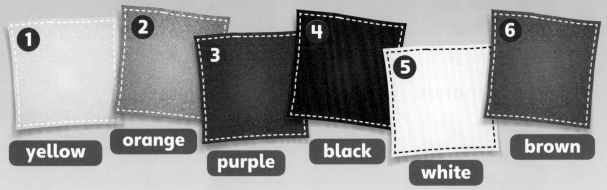

1 yellow **2** orange **3** purple **4** black **5** white **6** brown

---

85

25 **Listen and read. Then match and say.**

1 Brazil has got a green, yellow and blue flag.   **a**

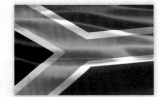

2 The green, white and orange flag is from Ireland.   **b**

3 South Africa has got a red, green, yellow, blue, black and white flag.   **c**

4 The flag from France is blue, white and red.   **d**

Ireland?

Green, white and orange.

26 **Look at 25. Read and circle.**

1 This flag is green, white and orange.　　**France / Ireland**
2 This flag is blue, green and yellow.　　**Brazil / France**
3 This flag is blue, yellow and black.　　**South Africa / Brazil**
4 This flag is blue, white and red.　　**France / Ireland**

27 **Look at 25. Ask and answer.**

How many flags have got green?

Three.

28 **Draw and colour your country's flag. Then talk with a partner.**

Where are you from?

I'm from France.

What colour is your flag?

It's red, white, and blue.

THINK BIG How many colours has your country's flag got? What flag has got the most colours?

29 **Listen and number. Then listen and repeat.**

Rinse with water. Dry your hands. Wash with soap.

30 **Listen and circle. Then match and sing.**

Keep Clean

1 Every day
   Before I eat
   And after I play,
   I **dry** / **wash** my hands.

2 With a lot of soap
   It's easy, you see.
   Rinse / **Dry** with water
   Just like me.

3 **Dry** / **Wash** them well and
   Sing this song.
   Keep your hands clean
   All day long!

a

b

c

THINK BIG **Do you wash your hands before you eat? Why?**

91
 31 **Listen, look and repeat.**

1 e　　　**2** c　　　**3** g　　　**4** m

92
 32 **Listen and find. Then say.**

cap　　　**map**　　　**pen**　　　**gas**

93
 33 **Listen and blend the sounds.**

1 p-e-t　pet　　**2** c-a-t　cat　　**3** g-e-t　get
4 m-a-t　mat　　**5** w-i-g　wig

94
 34 **Underline e, c, g and m. Then listen and chant.**

The cap is on the cat.
The cat goes on the map.
The pen goes on the bed.

96

35 **Complete the monster. Listen, draw and colour.**

36 **Draw your own monster. Ask and answer with a partner.**

 How many heads has it got?

It's got three heads!

97

37 **Listen and ✔.**

1 a   b

2 a   b

3 a   b

4 a   b

38 **Look and write. Use It's a, It's an and They're.**

ear
hands
mouth

1 _____
_____

2 _____
_____

3 _____
_____

I Can

☐ name one or more parts of the body.

☐ talk about my senses.

☐ say how I keep clean.

Do I Know It?

1 Look and circle. Practise.

😊 I know this. 😕 I don't know this.

1 p. 10

2 p. 14

3 p. 26

4 p. 30

5 p. 42

eye head
mouth nose
neck
hand arm
fingers
foot leg
toes

6 p. 46

98 99

2 **Get ready.**

A Listen and number.

B Look at **A** and point. Ask and answer.

What is it?   It's a backpack.

C Listen and circle.

1 Mark

2 Kate

D Look at **C** and point. Role play with a partner.

Who's she?   She's my sister.

3 **Get set.**

 Cut out the cards on page 181.
Now you're ready to **Go!**

4 **Go!**

A Listen. Put the cards on the numbers.

1	2	3
4	5	6

B Point to a card. Ask and answer.

Card 2. Has she got long hair?

Yes, she has.

5 **Write and draw.**

All About Me

My name is: _____

This is me.

This is my family.

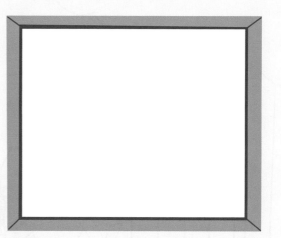

Do I Know It Now?

6 **Think about it.**

A Go to page 58. Look and circle again.

B Tick (✔).

☐ I can start the next unit.

☐ I can ask my teacher for help and then start the next unit.

☐ I can practise and then start the next unit.

7 **Rate this Checkpoint. Colour the stars.**

 easy hard

 fun ☆ not fun

Units 1–3 Exam Preparation

– Part A –

Listen and colour. There is one example.

– Part B –

Look and read. Put a tick (✔) or a cross (✗) in the box. There are two examples.

Examples

This is a pencil.   ✔

This is a book.   ✗

Questions

1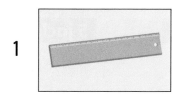

This is a ruler.

2

This is an eye.

3

This is a grandma. ☐

4

This is an ear.   ☐

5

This is a leg.   ☐

unit 4 My Favourite Clothes

1 Listen, look and say.

1 boots 2 dress 3 gloves 4 hat 5 jacket

6 trousers 7 blouse 8 shoes 9 skirt

10 T-shirt 11 socks 12 shirt 13 shorts

2 Listen, find and say.   3 Play a game.

4 Listen and chant. Then look at 1 and find.

What Are You Wearing?

What are you wearing?
I'm wearing a T-shirt.
What are you wearing?
I'm wearing a skirt.

What's he wearing?
He's wearing new shorts.
What's he wearing?
He's wearing old boots.

What's she wearing?
She's wearing a red hat.
What's she wearing?
She's wearing pink shoes.

106

5 Listen and number in order.

a  ☐

b  ☐

c ☐

d  ☐

e ☐

f ☐

g  ☐

h  ☐

6 Point, ask and answer.

What is it?

It's a pink T-shirt.

THINK BIG Look, think and say the clothes.

108
7 Listen and read. What colour is Patrick's hat?

8 Look and match.

1  **2**  **3**  **4**

a  **b**  **c**   **d**

THINK BIG Draw a funny hat. Then show the class.

9 Listen. Help Tim and Jane make sentences.

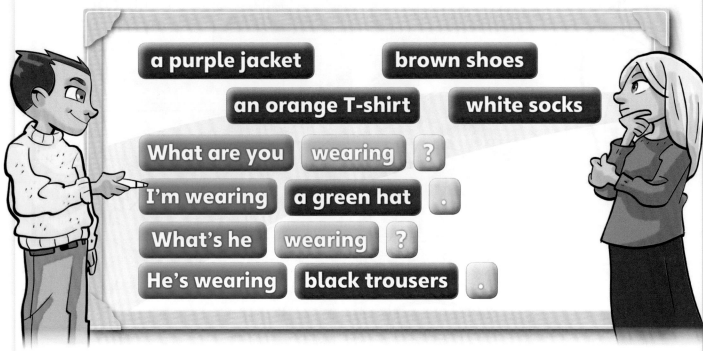

a purple jacket   brown shoes

an orange T-shirt   white socks

What are you   wearing   ?

I'm wearing   a green hat   .

What's he   wearing   ?

He's wearing   black trousers   .

10 Match. Then say. Use He's wearing or She's wearing.

1   2   3   4

a   b   c   d

11 **Listen and stick. Then say.**

12 **Role play with a partner.**

What are you wearing?

I'm wearing an orange T-shirt...

13 **What are you wearing? Draw and say.**

14 **Look, listen and repeat. Then say.**

1	2	3	4
hot	**wet**	**cold**	**dry**

5	6	7
mountains	**desert**	**jungle**

It's cold.

The mountains.

15 **Listen, read and point. Is it wet in the desert?**

The weather isn't the same everywhere. It's very cold in the mountains. It isn't hot. He's wearing his hat and gloves. It's very hot and dry in the desert. It isn't cold. She's wearing her shorts and hat. It's wet in the jungle. He's wearing his jacket and boots.

THINK BIG **Where is she? Draw and say.**

It's... I'm wearing...

16 **Look at 15. Read, circle and draw. Then say.**

1 It's **hot / cold** in the mountains. I'm wearing 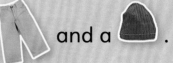 and a .

2 It's **dry / wet** in the desert. I'm wearing 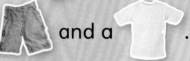 and a .

3 It's **cold / wet** in the jungle. I'm wearing 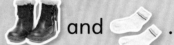 and .

4 It's **hot / cold** and **wet / dry** today. I'm wearing ☐ , ☐ and a ☐ .

17 **Look at 15. Play a game.**

What are you wearing?

I'm wearing a hat. It's cold.

You're in the mountains.   Yes.

PROJECT

18 **Make a Clothes poster. Then present it to the class.**

My Clothes

It's hot in the jungle.
I'm wearing a dress.

Grammar

19 **Look, listen and point. Then say.**

She's three.

a

b

c

Question	Answer
How old **are you**?	**I'm** seven.
How old **is he**?	**He's** four.
How old **is she**?	**She's** three.
How old **are they**?	**They're** eight.

20 **Read and match.**

1 How old is Penny?

2 How old are you?

3 How old are Pete and Max?

4 How old is Toprak?

a They're nine.

b He's ten.

c She's six.

d I'm eight.

21 **Read and write.**

He's   I'm   She's   They're

1 How old is she? _____ six.

2 How old are they? _____ seven.

3 How old is he? _____ nine.

4 How old are you? _____ ten.

Grammar

22 **Read, circle and find.**

1 How old **are you / are they**?

2 How old **is he / is she**?

3 How old **are they / are you**?

4 How old **is she / is he**?

8

4

10

6

23 **Read and circle. Then match and say.**

Today is my birthday. **Are you / I'm** nine. Selda is my sister.
He's / She's five. She's a little girl. I've got a baby brother.
He's / She's one. Erol is my best friend. **He's / She's** nine, too!
My grandparents are 70. They're very old!

1 How old are you?

2 How old is your brother?

3 How old is your sister?

4 How old are your grandparents?

1

5

70

9

24 **Draw yourself. Then write.**

This is me. I'm

_____ years old.

25 Look, listen and number. What hats have you got?

FUNNY HATS!

I've got a white cap and a purple woolly hat.

26 Listen, read and point. Why are some hats funny?

¹ This is Ascot. It's in England. Many people go and watch the horse races. They also look at the hats women are wearing.

² Some hats are very big and there are lots of colours. Red, blue, yellow and green.

³ Some hats have got very big flowers or long feathers. They're beautiful.

⁴ There are some very funny hats, too. They've got birds, horses, teacups and umbrellas on them! Do you wear funny hats?

27 **Look at 26. Read and circle.**

1 People watch the **horse** / **bird** races at Ascot.

2 Some hats have got very big **colours** / **flowers**.

3 Some hats have got long **feathers** / **birds**.

4 Some hats have got many **colours** / **races**.

5 Some hats are **funny** / **umbrellas**.

6 There are **women** / **teacups** on some of the hats.

28 **Draw yourself wearing a funny hat. Then talk with a partner.**

My hat has got dogs on it.

What a funny hat!

THINK BIG **When do you wear a funny hat? Tell a friend.**

120

29 Listen and number. Then say.

a

b

c

They're wearing traditional clothes from Guatemala.

They're wearing traditional clothes from the Philippines.

They're wearing traditional clothes from Kenya.

30 Look at 29. Ask and answer.

What are they wearing?

They're wearing big hats and blue dresses.

THINK BIG Do people wear traditional clothes in your country? What do they wear?

31 **Listen, look and repeat.**

1 o   **2** k   **3** ck

32 **Listen and find. Then say.**

kid   **sock**   **on**

33 **Listen and blend the sounds.**

1 p-o-t   pot   **2** k-i-t   kit   **3** n-e-ck neck
4 k-i-ck kick   **5** d-o-g dog   **6** p-i-ck pick

34 **Underline o, k and ck. Then listen and chant.**

Put on your socks,
Put on your kit.
Kick the ball,
Kick, kick, kick!

35 **Work in two pairs. Ask and answer.**

36 **Work in two groups. One group looks away and answers the teacher. Score 1 point for each correct answer.**

Take turns. Which group remembers the most?

126
37 **Listen and ✔.**

1 a  ☐

b  ☐

c ☐

2 a  ☐

b  ☐

c ☐

3 a  ☐

b  ☐

c  ☐

4 a  ☐

b  ☐

c  ☐

38 **Look and write. Use How old.**

 1 _____ _____ They're eight.

 2 _____ _____ He's five.

I Can

☐ say what people are wearing and their age.

☐ talk about clothes.

☐ respect all cultures.

unit 5

Busy at Home

128
1 Listen, look and say.

1 brushing my teeth

2 drinking

3 combing my hair

4 reading

5 having a bath

6 making lunch

7 washing

8 getting dressed

9 sleeping

10 playing

11 talking on the phone

12 eating

129
2 Listen, find and say.   **3** Play a game.

4 Listen and sing. Then look at 1 and find.

What Are You Doing?

I'm brushing my teeth.
I'm combing my hair.
I'm busy. I'm busy.
What are you doing?

I'm eating my breakfast.
I'm washing my face.
I'm busy. I'm busy.
What are you doing?

I'm talking on the phone.
I'm making my lunch.
I'm busy. I'm busy.
What are you doing?

Chorus

132

5 Listen and say yes or no.

1  **2**  **3**

6 Look at 5. Ask and answer.

What are you doing?

I'm eating.

You're Number 1!

 THINK BIG Why do we brush our teeth?
Why do we sleep?

Story

7 **Listen and read. What's Patrick drawing?**

8 Look at the story. Circle.

1 Who is playing?

2 Who is making lunch?

3 Who is drawing?

THINK BIG Draw a picture for your mum. Say.

135

9 Listen. Help Tim and Jane make sentences.

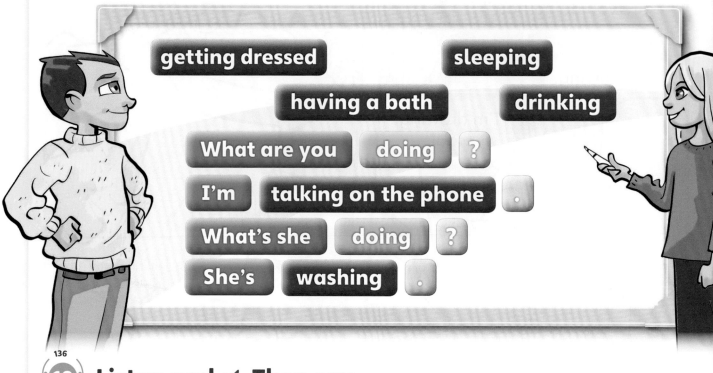

getting dressed   sleeping

having a bath   drinking

What are you   doing   ?

I'm   talking on the phone   .

What's she   doing   ?

She's   washing   .

136

10 Listen and ✔. Then say.

1 What's she doing?
a   b

2 What's he doing?
a   b

3 What's he doing?
a   b

4 What's she doing?
a   b

138

11 Listen and stick. Then say.

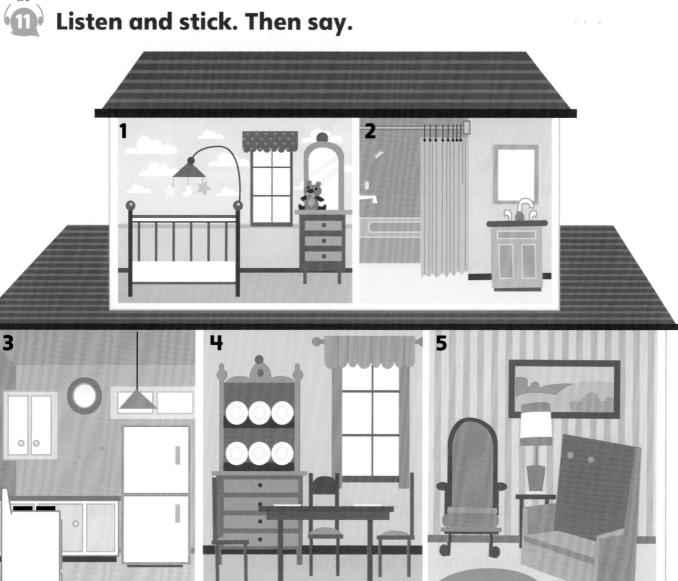

12 Look at 11. Ask and answer.

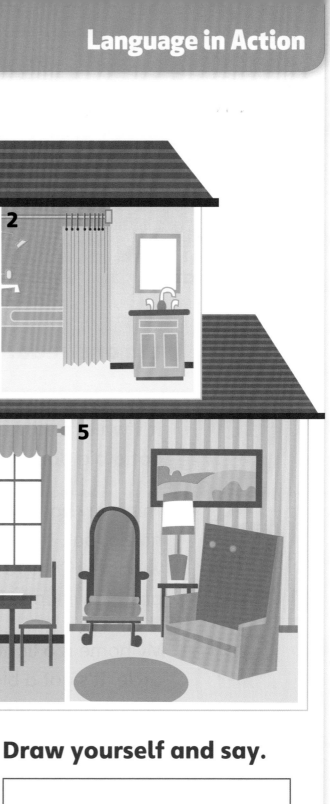

What's she doing?

She's sleeping.

13 Draw yourself and say.

139

14 Look, listen and repeat. Then point and say.

1 flat   **2 yurt**   **3 houseboat**   **4 lighthouse**

> It's a houseboat.

 140

15 Look, listen and read. What shapes are there?

1 My home is a yurt. It's a circle. It's white and very big. It's got a big door.

2 This is my home. It's a houseboat. It's got two small windows. They're circles. It's got one big window. It's a square.

3 My home is a lighthouse. It's a circle. It's got a big door. The door is a rectangle.

4 This is my home. It's a flat. It's in a tall building. It's got big windows. They're rectangles.

THINK BIG Find and draw a picture of one of these houses. What shapes can you see?
a igloo   **b** hut   **c** teepee

16 **Look at 15. Read and match.**

1 My home is a white circle. It's got two small windows.

2 My home has got a big door. It's a rectangle.

3 My home has got big windows. They're rectangles.

4 My home has got one big window. It's a square.

a houseboat

b flat

c lighthouse

d yurt

17 **Look at 15. Play a game.**

It's got two small windows. They're circles.

Yes.

It's a houseboat.

PROJECT

18 **Make a House Shapes poster. Then present it to the class.**

My house is a square. It's got two windows. They're circles. The door is a rectangle.

19 **Look, listen and point. Then say.**

a

b

c

d

It's small.
It's white.

It's...	They're...
It's brown and white.	They're yellow.
It's big.	They're small.
What colour is it?	What colour are they?

20 **Read and match.**

1 It's brown
and white.

2 They're yellow.

What colour is it?

3 They're black
and brown.

What colour are they?

4 It's white.

5 It's pink.

6 They're red
and green.

21 **Read and circle.**

1 What colour **is it / are they**?   They're orange and red.

2 What colour is it?   **It's / They're** grey and white.

3 What colour are they?   **It's / They're** pink and blue.

4 What colour **is it / are they**?   It's purple.

22 **Look, read and write.**

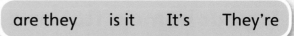

are they   is it   It's   They're

1 What colour is it?
_____ red.

2 What colour are they?
_____ blue and yellow.

3 What colour _____?
It's blue and white.

4 What colour _____?
They're red, green, yellow and blue.

23 **Read and draw.**

The Haunted House.

This is a haunted house. It's got three ghosts. They're white. Boo!

The door is tall. It's brown. Bang!

The window is big. The curtains are red. They're long. Whoosh!

The house has got a black cat. It's big. It's scary. Meow!

24 **Look around your classroom. Ask and answer with a partner.**

What colour is it?

What colour are they?

It's white. The desk is white.

They're red and green. The pens are red and green.

25 Is your home a flat or a house? Talk about it.

Homes

My home is a flat. It's big. It's got five rooms. It's got big windows.

143

26 Listen and read. Where do Mum and Dad sleep?

1 This is my home. It's a caravan. It's on a caravan site.

2 It's got a kitchen but it hasn't got a dining room. The kitchen has got a small table. It's a square. The kitchen has got four chairs.

3 The living room has got a big TV. It's a rectangle.

4 My home has got two bedrooms. My mum and dad sleep in the big bedroom. My bedroom is small but it's got a big window.

5 The bathroom is small, too. It's got a small window. It's a circle.

6 My caravan isn't very big but it's very comfortable. My family is happy here.

27 Look at 26. Read and circle.

1 This is my home. It's a **caravan** / **flat**.

2 It hasn't got a **kitchen** / **dining room**.

3 The kitchen has got four **tables** / **chairs**.

4 The TV is a **rectangle** / **square**.

5 Mum and Dad sleep in the **small** / **big** bedroom.

6 The bathroom has got a **small** / **big** window.

28 Look at 26. Play a game.

It's got a big TV. It's a rectangle.

The living room.

29 Draw a caravan for you. Talk with a partner.

My caravan has got a small kitchen and two bedrooms.

THINK BIG Why do some people live in a caravan? Talk about it.

145

30 **Listen and match. Then listen and repeat.**

She's helping her parents.   She's cleaning her room.
She's drying the dishes.   He's washing the dishes.

1

2

3

4

31 **How do you help at home? Act it out. Your partner guesses.**

He's drying the dishes.

THINK BIG **Does it feel good to help at home? Why?**

147
32 **Listen, look and repeat.**

1 u   **2** f   **3** ff

148
33 **Listen and find. Then say.**

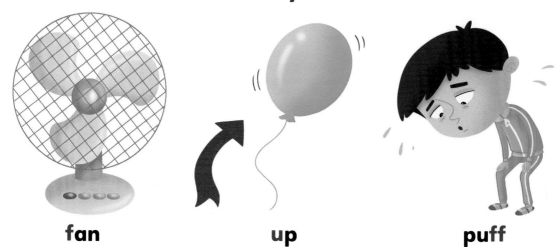

fan   up   puff

149
34 **Listen and blend the sounds.**

1 r-u-n   run   **2** f-u-n   fun   **3** o-ff   off
4 s-u-n   sun   **5** f-o-g   fog

150
35 **Underline u, f and ff. Then listen and chant.**

We're having fun,
Running in the sun.
Up, up, up!
Puff, puff, puff!

36 Work in groups. Play the Memory game.

Pupil 1: Act and say.

Pupil 2: Talk about Pupil 1. Then act and say.

I'm eating.

She's eating.
I'm reading.

She's eating.
He's reading.
I'm washing.

Pupil 3: Talk about Pupils 1 and 2. Then act and say.

Play with the whole class. How much can you remember?

152

37 Listen and number.

a

b

c

d

e

38 Look and match.

1 It's red.   **2** They're white.   **3** It's green.   **4** They're small.

a

b

c

d

I Can

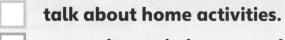

☐ talk about home activities.

☐ name shapes in homes and describe things.

☐ talk about helping at home.

unit 6

On the Farm

153

1 Listen, look and say.

1 cat

2 dog

3 cow

4 sheep

5 turtle

6 horse

7 duck

8 frog

9 chicken

10 goat

154

2 Listen, find and say.   **3** Play a game.

4 **Listen and chant. Then look at 1 and find.**

Look at the Animals

Look over here!
Look over there!
There are animals
Everywhere!

What is it?
It's a duck.
What's it doing?
It's flying up high!

What is it?
It's a dog!
What's it doing?
It's jumping with the frogs!

What are they?
They're goats!
What are they doing?
They're eating some oats!

Chorus

5 **Listen and number.**

a

b

c

6 **Look at 5. Ask and answer.**

What is it?

It's a horse.

What's it doing?

It's running.

THINK BIG **What animals can jump?**
What animals can fly?

song/vocabulary Unit 6 **97**

159
7 **Listen and read. What's the goat doing?**

8 Look and number.

1 running   **2** flying   **3** eating   **4** jumping

a

b

c

d

THINK BIG What happens next? Draw.

160

9 Listen. Help Tim and Jane make sentences.

cow   turtle   frogs

jumping   sleeping   drinking

What's the   goat   doing   ?

It's   eating   .

What are the   chickens   doing   ?

They're   running   .

161

10 Listen and ✔.

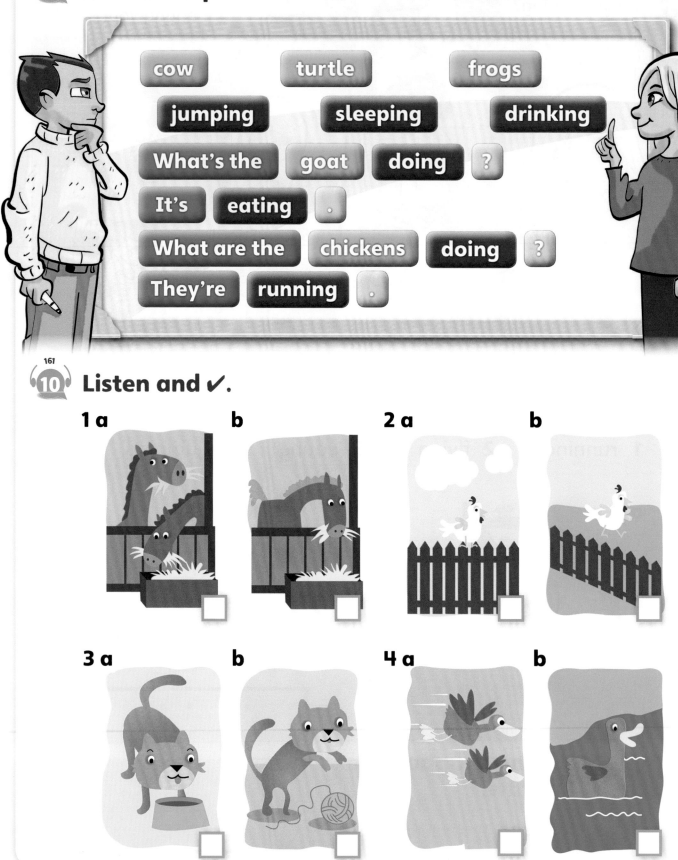

1 a   b   2 a   b

3 a   b   4 a   b

11 **Listen and stick. Then say.**

12 **Look at 11. Ask and answer.**

What's the horse doing?

It's eating.

13 **Colour and say. What are the animals doing?**

14 **Look, listen and repeat. Then match.**

164

1 chick

2 puppy

3 kitten

4 calf

a It's got black ears.

b It's black and white.

c It's got blue eyes.

d It's yellow.

15 **Look, listen and read. How many baby animals are ther**

165

1 Look at the cows. The big cow is brown. She's got a baby cow. A baby cow is called a calf.

2 The big dog is happy. Look at her baby dogs. Baby dogs are called puppies.

3 This chicken is very big. Look at the baby chickens. They're called chicks.

4 Look at the cats. There's one big cat and three baby cats. Baby cats are called kittens.

THINK BIG **Read and match.**

chick   kitten   puppy   calf

dog   chicken   cow   cat

16 Listen and number. Then say.

167

a

A baby chicken is called a...

b

A baby dog is called a...

c

A baby cat is called a...

d

A baby cow is called a...

17 Look at 15. Play a game.

What are baby dogs called?

Baby dogs are called puppies.

PROJECT

18 Make a Baby Animals poster. Then present it to the class.

Baby Animals

a kitten

a calf

a puppy

These are my baby animals. I've got a kitten, a calf and a puppy.

19 **Look, listen and number.**

a

b

c

d

my	This is my dog.	its	This is its mum.
your	Is this your dog?	our	These are our chickens.
his	His name's Patch.	your	These are your animals.
her	Her name's Misha.	their	They're eating their food.

20 **Read and match. Then say. Use This is or These are.**

1 Pete   a her puppy

2 me   b his cat   This is his cat.

3 Patty   c our goats

4 Dad, me and Mum   d my turtle

5 the kitten   e your chickens

6 you and Sally   f their kittens

7 my brothers   g its mum

21 Read and write. | her   his   my   their   your |

1 She's got a tennis ball. It's _____ ball.

2 I've got a brother and a sister. They're _____ family.

3 He's got a toy spaceship. It's _____ spaceship.

4 They've got a pet. It's _____ dog.

5 You've got an old car. It's _____ car.

**22 Play a game. Who is it? Take turns.
A: Describe a person in your class.
B: Listen to A. Who is it?**

His hair is very short. His eyes are blue. His T-shirt is black. His shoes are red.

Is it Mehmet?

Yes, it is.

23 Circle and write. Then draw.

This is my class. Our teacher is a
man / woman. **His / Her** name's
_____.

This is my best friend. **His / Her**
name's _____.

These are my classmates. **Their /
Our** names are _____ and
_____.

24 Have you got a pet? What's its name? What colour is it?

Pets

170
25 Listen and read. What colours are the pets?

1  **2**  **3**  **4**

1 I'm Sharon. I'm from Australia. This is my pet hamster. He's brown. His name's Charlie.

2 My name's Reiko. I'm from Japan. I've got a pet canary. He's yellow. His name's Tom Bird.

3 Hi. My name's Zack. I'm from the United States. I've got a pet snake. She's green. Her name's Samantha.

4 I'm Elina. I'm from Greece. This is my pet mouse. She's very small. She's white. Her name's Zoe.

26 **Look at 25. Read, circle and write.**

1 Zack has got a **mouse / snake**. Her name's _____.

2 Sharon has got a **hamster / canary**. His name's _____.

3 Elina has got a **mouse / hamster**. Her name's _____.

4 Reiko has got a **snake / canary**. His name's _____.

27 **Draw a pet for you. Then describe your pet to a partner.**

I'm Bahar. I'm from Turkey. This is my pet cat. She's...

THINK BIG **Which animals make good pets? Which animals make bad pets?**

Listen and find the picture. Then listen and repeat.

172

1 feeding

2 walking

3 brushing

4 playing

 Look at 28. Role play with a partner.

What are you doing?

I'm feeding the chicks.

THINK BIG **How are you kind to animals? Draw.**

30 **Listen, look and repeat.**

1 r   **2** h   **3** j

31 **Listen and find. Then say.**

  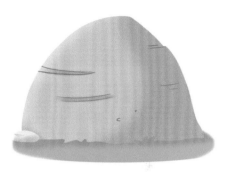

hat   **jam**   **rock**

32 **Listen and blend the sounds.**

1 r-e-d   red   **2** h-e-n   hen   **3** j-e-t   jet
4 r-u-n   run   **5** h-u-t   hut   **6** j-o-b   job

33 **Underline r, h and j. Then listen and chant.**

A red hen in
A red hat
Is eating red jam.
Run, red hen, run!

179

Listen, find and say. Then role play.

1

2

3

4

35 ## Work in teams. Role play. Ask and answer.

What's the dog doing?

It's jumping.

36 **Look and match.**

a

b

1 eating

2 flying

3 jumping

4 running

c

d

180
37 **Listen and number.**

a

b

c

d

38 **Read and circle.**

1 This is my dad. **His / Her** name's Erol.

2 Emma is here. **Her / My** school is closed.

3 These are our dogs. **Our / Their** ears are big.

4 I've got short hair. **Your / My** hair is black.

I Can

☐ talk about what animals and baby animals are doing.

☐ talk about possessions.

☐ say how to be kind to animals.

1 **Look and circle. Practise.**

☺ I know this.   ☹ I don't know this.

181

2 **Get ready.**

A Look. Circle the correct words.

1 Mum is **reading a book / eating**.
2 Dad is **washing / making lunch**.
3 The cat is **sleeping / playing**.
4 The girl is **drinking / talking on the phone**.

B Look at **A** and point. Ask and answer.

What's she wearing?

She's wearing a green shirt and brown trousers.

C Listen and number.

a   b   c   d

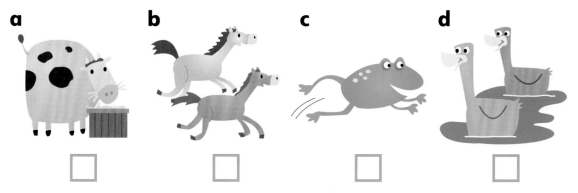

☐   ☐   ☐   ☐

3 Get set.

✂ **STEP 1** Cut out the cards on page 183.

▢ **STEP 2** Put the cards on your desk. Mix the cards up. Now you're ready to **Go!**

4 Go!

A Arrange the cards to make the person below. Ask and answer with a partner.

- What's she wearing?
- What's she doing?

B Make 3 more people. Don't show your cards. Describe one of your people. Your partner makes the same person. Show your cards and check.

> He's in the bathroom. He's talking on the phone...

5 **Draw.**

All About Me

My favourite animal is:

I'm wearing:

Do I Know It Now?

6 **Think about it.**

A Go to page 112. Look and circle again.

B Tick (✔).

☐ I can start the next unit.

☐ I can ask my teacher for help and then start the next unit.

☐ I can practise and then start the next unit.

7 **Rate this Checkpoint. Colour the stars.**

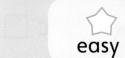
easy   hard

fun   not fun

Units 4–6 Exam Preparation

– Part A –

 Look at the pictures. Now listen and look. There is one example.

Which is Sue?

 A ✔

 B ☐

 C ☐

1 What's Tom doing?

 A ☐

 B ☐

 C ☐

2 Which is Mum?

 A ☐

 B ☐

 C ☐

3 What's in his backpack?

 A ☐

 B ☐

 C ☐

4 What's Anna doing?

 A ☐

 B ☐

 C ☐

5 What's Tom wearing?

 A ☐

 B ☐

 C ☐

Look at the pictures. Look at the letters. Write the words.

Example

c a t

t c a

Questions

1

_ _ _

w o c

2

_ _ _ _

g o d

3

_ _ _ _

a t o g

4

_ _ _ _

o r f g

5

_ _ _ _ _ _

l e t u t r

unit 7

Party Time

183

1 Listen, look and say.

1 cake

2 fruit

3 ice cream

4 juice

5 milk

6 water

7 pizza

8 salad

9 chicken

10 chips

11 pasta

184

2 Listen, find and say.

3 Play a game.

185 186

4 Listen and sing. Then look at 1 and find.

It's My Party!

Welcome, friends.
Please sit down.
It's time for my party!
With games and a clown!

I've got pizza, chicken,
Salad, too.
Fruit, cake
And ice cream for you!

Or put some pasta
On your plate.
With juice or milk
It sure tastes great.

Thanks for the presents.
What a great day!
Let's eat and drink
And play, play, play. (x2)

187

5 Listen and say yes or no.

1  2  3  4

6 Look at 5. Ask and answer.

 What's he got?

He's got milk.

THINK BIG What food do you eat every day?
What food do you eat on special days?

189
7 **Listen and read. What day is Tim's party?**

8 Look at the story. Read and circle.

1 Tim's got...   a    b

2 Jane's got...   a    b

3 What's Patrick got?   a    b

THINK BIG **What day is it today? Circle and say.**

Monday   Tuesday   Wednesday   Thursday   Friday   Saturday   Sunday

Language in Action

190

9 Listen. Help Tim and Jane make sentences.

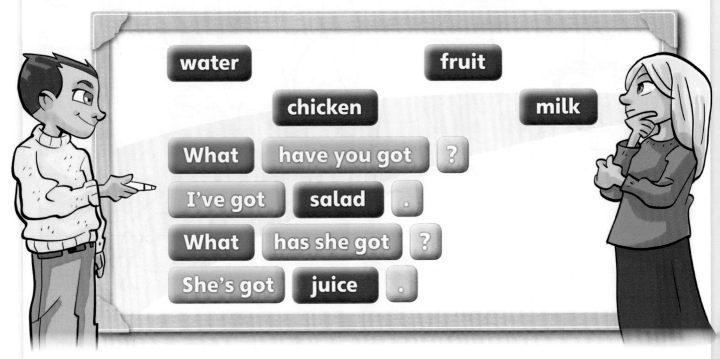

water   fruit

chicken   milk

What   have you got   ?

I've got   salad   .

What   has she got   ?

She's got   juice   .

10 Match. Then say.

1 What have you got?
I've got salad.

2 What have you got?
I've got cake and milk.

a    b

3 What have you got?
I've got juice and ice cream.

4 What have you got?
I've got fruit.

c    d

191

11 **Listen and stick. Then say.**

12 **Look at 11. Ask and answer.**

What's she got?

She's got fruit.

13 **What have you got?**
Draw and say.

192
 14 **Look, listen and repeat. Then say.**

1 sugar

2 chocolate

3 biscuits

4 salt

5 crisps

6 chips

I've got chocolate and chips.

193
 15 **Listen, read and point. Is pizza sweet? Is cake salty?**

Sweet   Salty

1 Food can be sweet or salty. Sweet food has got sugar in it. Chocolate and biscuits are sweet. Cake is sweet, too. They've got sugar in them. My favourite sweet food is chocolate.

2 Crisps have got salt in them. Pizza and chips have salt in them, too. They're all salty. My favourite salty food is pizza.

 THINK BIG **Name other sweet and salty foods. What's your favourite? Salty or sweet?**

16 **Look at 15. Circle T for true and F for false.**

1 Chocolate is sweet.   T F

2 Biscuits are salty.   T F

3 Crisps are salty.   T F

4 Chips are sweet.   T F

5 Cake is sweet.   T F

194

17 **Look and match. Then listen and check.**

sweet   salty

PROJECT

18 **Make a Sweet and Salty Food poster. Then present it to the class.**

sweet   salty

This is my food poster. Chocolate is sweet. Chips are salty.

19 Look, listen and read. Then say.

196

1 I don't go to school on Sunday. I don't get up early.

2 My mum doesn't go to work. She doesn't clean the house every day.

3 My dad doesn't go to work. He doesn't watch TV all day.

4 My big sisters don't go to school. They don't study all afternoon.

5 The dog doesn't sleep in its basket. It doesn't let me sleep!

She doesn't go to school.

I/You/We/They		
I		go to school.
You	don't	do your homework.
We		eat cake.
They		study all afternoon.

He/She/It		
He		sleep in a chair.
She	doesn't	go to work.
It		let me sleep.

20 **Read and circle.**

1 I **doesn't** / **don't** eat drink juice.

2 He **don't** / **doesn't** watch TV in bed.

3 We **don't** / **doesn't** listen to music in class.

4 They **doesn't** / **don't** eat in the car.

5 She **doesn't** / **don't** have a shower every day.

6 You **don't** / **do** sleep on your desk.

21 **Read and write don't or doesn't.**

1 Paul _____ run in class.

2 Mike and Pete _____ drink juice for lunch.

3 Batu and Asya _____ play football.

4 The girls _____ wear trousers at school.

5 Alex and I _____ walk to school.

6 My brother _____ eat salad.

22 **Make three silly sentences. Tell your partner.**

I sing with my toes.

You don't sing with your toes.

23 **What food do you have on your birthday? What's your favourite?**

Birthday Food

> My favourite food is pizza.

197

24 **Listen and read. What food do the children have on their birthdays?**

Mexico

1 My name's Miguel. In Mexico, I have a piñata with sweets on my birthday. It's my favourite day.

2 I'm Jack. I live in the United States. I have a big cake on my birthday. It's very sweet.

3 I'm Susie from South Korea. I have seaweed soup on my birthday. It's salty.

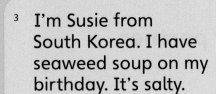

United States

Korea

4 I'm Anya. I'm from Russia. On my birthday, I have a big fruit pie. It's my favourite sweet cake.

Russia

25 Look at 24. Read and write.

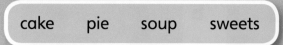
cake   pie   soup   sweets

1 _____   2 _____   3 _____   4 _____

26 Look at 24. Read and circle. Then say.

1 Miguel doesn't have **cake** / **sweets**.

2 Jack doesn't have **soup** / **cake**.

3 Susie doesn't have **pie** / **soup**

4 Anya doesn't have **cake** / **pie**.

27 Write about you. Then tell a partner.

My name's _____. On my birthday, I have

_____, _____

and _____.

TH:NK BIG Why do people have special food on their birthday? How else do they celebrate?

28 **Look and number in order. Then listen and check.**

a

b

c

I eat lunch
every day.

I eat dinner
every day.

I eat breakfast
every day.

29 **Read and match. Then draw and say.**

1 My brother eats salad for lunch
every day.

a

2 Mum drinks milk for breakfast
every day.

b

3 Dad eats chicken for dinner
every day.

c

4 I eat...

d

THINK BIG **Do you eat three meals every day?
Why do you think it is important?**

200
 30 **Listen, look and repeat.**

1 l   **2** ll   **3** v   **4** w

201
31 **Listen and find. Then say.**

| **web** | **doll** | **leg** | **van** |

202
 32 **Listen and blend the sounds.**

1 l-e-t   let   **2** b-e-ll   bell   **3** v-e-t   vet
4 w-e   we   **5** w-i-n   win   **6** t-a-ll   tall

203
33 **Underline l, ll, v and w. Then listen and chant.**

Let's ring the bell
For the vet
With the van!

205

34 Find the differences and say. Then listen and check.

Mum

Sam

Dad

Sally

Suzie

Picture A

Mum

Sam

Dad

Sally

Suzie

Picture B

35 Look at 34. Play a game.

In Picture A, Sam's got ice cream.

In Picture B, Sam's got fruit.

207
36 **Listen and circle.**

1 a    b    c

2 a    b    c

3 a    b    c

4 a    b    c

37 **Read and circle.**

1 She **doesn't** / **don't** walk to school.
2 They **doesn't** / **don't** eat biscuits.
3 I **doesn't** / **don't** play with puppets.
4 We **don't** / **doesn't** like basketball.

I Can

☐ talk about party food.
☐ ask and answer about what people have got.
☐ name sweet and salty food.

Fun and Games

208
1 🎧 Listen, look and say.

1 action figure

2 plane

3 ball

4 bike

5 blocks

6 cars

7 stuffed animal

8 doll

9 game

10 puppet

11 train

209
2 🎧 Listen, find and say.   **3** 💬 Play a game.

4 **Listen and sing. Then look at and find.**

What's in Your Toy Box?

Kim, what's in your toy box?
Have you got a plane?
No, but this is my blue car.
And where's my grey train?

Kim, what's on your toy shelf?
Have you got a ball?
Yes, yes, here it is.
And here's my purple doll.

Kim, what's on your table?
Have you got big blocks?
Yes, and these are my puppets.
My favourite's Mr Fox!

These are my favourite toys,
Purple, green and grey.
I share my toys with my friends.
And I play every day!

213

5 **Listen and number.**

a   b   c

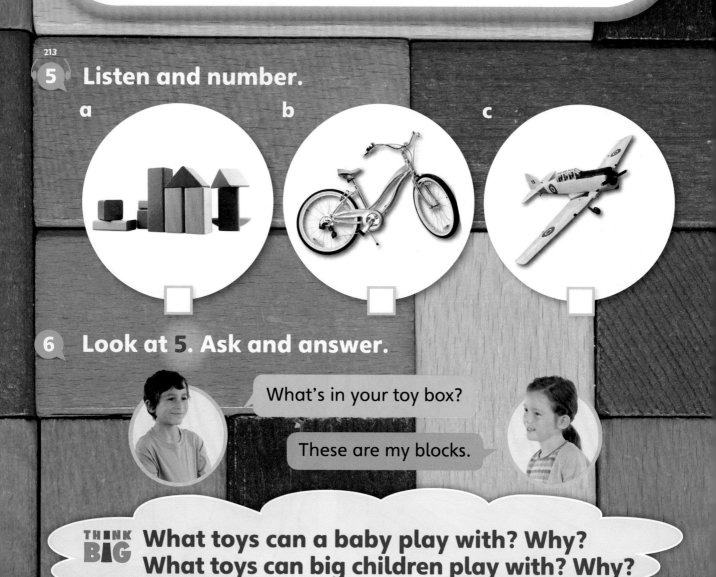

6 **Look at 5. Ask and answer.**

What's in your toy box?

These are my blocks.

THINK BIG **What toys can a baby play with? Why?**
What toys can big children play with? Why?

215

 Listen and read. Where is Jane's doll?

Where Are My Toys?

Where's my bike, Dad?

Sorry, Jane. No riding your bike today. It's very cold.

1

Where's my ball, Dad?

Sorry. No playing with your ball in the house.

2

Dad, where's my doll?

It's under the table, Jane.

3

Oh, and where are my action figures?

4

8 Look at the story and circle.

1 Jane's doll is under the

a 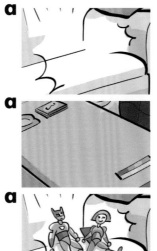 b 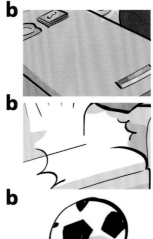 .

2 Jane's action figures are on the

a b .

3 Jane is playing with her

a  b  .

THINK BIG What's your favourite toy?
Where is your favourite toy?

216

9 Listen. Help Tim and Jane make sentences.

| on the shelf | under the table |
| plane | stuffed animals |

Where's the ball ?

It's in the toy box .

Where are the blocks ?

They're under the sofa .

217

10 Listen and ✔.

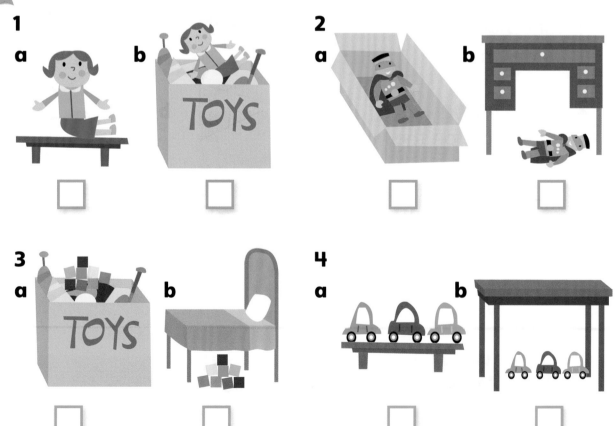

1
a   b

2
a   b

3
a   b

4
a   b

11 Listen and stick. Then say.

12 Look at 11. Ask and answer.

Where are the dolls?

They're under the table.

**13 Colour and say.
Where are the toys?**

14 **Have you got a kite? What does it look like?**

> I've got a kite. My kite is big. It's colourful.

 15 **Look, listen and read. Then match.**

There are many kite flying festivals in Japan. The kites look like different animals. People fly their kites high in the sky. The best kite wins. Let's look at some.

1 This kite looks like a dragon.
It's red, black and yellow.
It's long and colourful.

a

2 This kite looks like a bird.
It's blue and orange.
It's high in the sky.

b

3 This kite looks like a butterfly.
It's green. It's very big.

c

4 This kite looks like a fish.
It's orange. It's got a long tail.

d

 THINK BIG Find a picture of a kite. What colour is it? What does it look like?

16 **Look at 15. Read and write.**

> big   bird   fish   red

1 This kite looks like a butterfly. It's green. It's very _____.

2 This kite looks like a _____. It's orange. It's got a long tail.

3 This kite looks like a dragon. It's _____, black and yellow. It's long and colourful.

4 This kite looks like a _____. It's blue and orange. It's high in the sky.

17 **Look at 15. Play a game.**

It's orange. It's got a long tail.

Picture c. The fish kite.

PROJECT

18 **Make a Cool Kite. Then present it to the class.**

This is my kite. It looks like a fish. It's yellow. It's got a long tail.

221

19 **Look, listen and point. Then say.**

There is salad.

There are sandwiches.

There is a pizza.	There are sandwiches.
There isn't a cake.	There aren't chips.
Is there a salad?	Are there sandwiches?
Yes, there is. No, there isn't.	Yes, there are. No, there aren't.

20 **Read and circle.**

1 There **is / are** ten books on the shelf.

2 There **is / are** eight cats in the basket.

3 There **is / are** a ball under the sofa.

4 There **is / are** a shoe on the bed.

5 There **is / are** twelve cars in the toy box.

6 There **is / are** a marker pen on the desk.

21 **Look and ✔.**

1 Are there balls? Yes, there are. ☐ No, there aren't. ☐

2 Is there an action
figure? Yes, there is. ☐ Yes, there are. ☐

3 Is there a stuffed
animal? No, there aren't. ☐ Yes, there is. ☐

4 Are there cars? No, there aren't. ☐ Yes, there are. ☐

5 Is there a plane? Yes, there is. ☐ No, there isn't. ☐

6 Are there skates? No, there isn't. ☐ Yes, there are. ☐

22 **Read and match.**

1 Is there a   **a** egg in the box?

2 Are there   **b** fish on the shelf?

3 Is there an   **c** oranges in the basket?

4 There is a   **d** six pies on the desk.

5 There are   **e** glass of milk on the table.

23 **Ask and answer about your toys.**

Is there a doll on your bed?

Yes, there is.

Are there blocks in your toy box?

No, there aren't.

24 **How many toys have you got? What's your favourite?**

> I've got a lot of toys. My favourite is my plane. It's grey.

222

25 **Listen, read and point. How many toys has Emma got?**

My Toy Box

> This is my toy box.
> There are toys in it.

1   I like my plane and my train. The plane is red, blue and white. It's from the U.K. The train is wooden. It's from China.

2   My favourite toys are my dolls. They're from Russia. There is a big doll and there are small dolls in it. The small dolls go into the big doll. The last doll is a baby. The dolls are colourful. I love my Russian dolls. I play with them every day.

26 **Circle T for true and F for false.**

1 The plane is from China.	**T F**
2 The Russian dolls are from Japan.	**T F**
3 There are small dolls in the big Russian doll.	**T F**
4 The small dolls go in the big doll.	**T F**
5 Emma's got a train from the U.K.	**T F**

27 **Look at 25. Read and circle.**

1 This is my **small / toy** box.

2 The plane is red, blue and **white / grey**.

3 The train is **Russian / wooden**.

4 The last doll is a **baby / toy**.

5 Emma's got one **big / small** doll.

6 The plane is from **China / the U.K.**

28 **Draw Russian dolls for you. Talk with a partner.**

What colour are your dolls?

They're green and yellow.

How many small dolls are in the big doll?

Six.

THINK BIG **Has your country got a special toy? What is it?**

29 Listen and find the picture. Then listen and repeat.

1

2

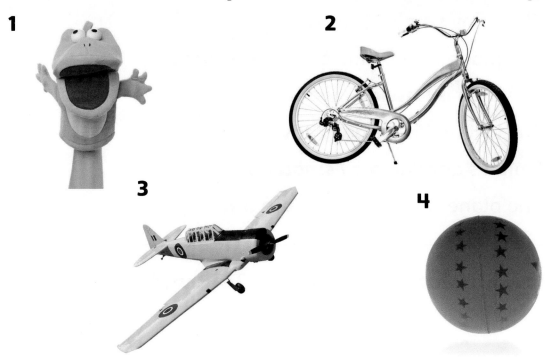

3

4

30 Look and number. Then say.

a

Sharing is fun!

b

Here's my car.
Let's share.

c

Okay. Thank you!

THINK BIG Is it good to share your toys?
Why?

225
31 **Listen, look and repeat.**

1 qu   **2** x   **3** y

226
32 **Listen and find. Then say.**

yell   **quick**   **six**

227
33 **Listen and blend the sounds.**

1 qu-a-ck   quack   **2** b-o-x   box   **3** y-e-s   yes
4 o-x   ox   **5** f-o-x   fox   **6** y-u-m   yum

228
34 **Underline qu, x and y. Then listen and chant.**

Six quick foxes,
In a yellow box!

230
35 **Listen and circle. Then say.**

36 **Look at 35. Ask and answer.**

Where are the action figures?

They're on the bed and under the chair.

Where are the planes?

They're on the shelf and under the desk.

37 **Look and match.**

1 blocks

2 bike

3 cars

4 game

5 puppet

6 train

a

b

c

d

e

f

38 **Read and match.**

1 There's   **a** in the backpack.

2 There are ten   **b** two shoes under the desk.

3 There are   **c** salad on the table?

4 There's an   **d** a puppet on the bed.

5 There aren't pens   **e** egg in the box.

6 Is there a   **f** balls on the shelf.

I Can

☐ **name toys.**

☐ **say where something is.**

☐ **talk about sharing my toys.**

unit 9 Play Time

1 Listen, look and say.

1 catching

2 throwing

3 hitting

4 kicking

5 dancing

6 singing

7 skating

8 riding

9 skipping

2 Listen, find and say. **3** Play a game.

4 Listen and sing. Then look at 1 and find.

Play Time Is Cool!

We like play time at our school.
Skipping and dancing,
Throwing and catching.
Play time is cool at our school!

I'm throwing the ball.
It's so much fun!
Are you
Hitting and running?
Yes, and it's fun.

We're kicking the ball
And trying to score.
It's so much fun.
Let's play some more.

Chorus

5 Listen and ✔.

1 a 　b 　　2 a 　b

6 Look at 5. Ask and answer.

　Are you kicking?

Yes, I am.　

THINK BIG Look at 1. What are they doing with their feet? What are they doing with their hands?

238

7 **Listen and read. What's Ann doing?**

8 Look at the story. Number the pictures in order.

a  ☐

b  ☐

c  ☐

d  ☐

THINK BIG **Imagine you are getting ready for bed. Act it out and say what you are doing!**

239
9 Listen. Help Tim and Jane make sentences.

skipping   throwing

skating   riding

Is she singing ?

Yes, she is .

Are they dancing ?

No, they aren't .

240
10 Listen and number.

a

b

c

d

e

f

11 Listen and stick. Then say.

12 Look at 11. Ask and answer.

Is he running?

No, he isn't.
He's skipping.

13 Draw and say. Are you throwing a ball?

243
Listen, repeat and find. Then ask and answer.

> What games do you play in the playground?

> Hopscotch and skipping.

 244
Listen, read and point. What's her favourite game?

climbing

skipping

hide and seek

hopscotch

tag

1 Playing games with my friends is a lot of fun. We play in the school playground every day.

2 We climb to the top of the bars. Up! Up! Up! We also skip. My friends skip very fast. Jump! Jump! Jump!

3 We play hide and seek, too. I count to ten, then I look for my friends. 1, 2, 3... Where are you?

4 We also play hopscotch. Hop, hop, hop!

5 My favourite game of all is tag. Let's run! Run! Run! Tag, you're it!

 THINK BIG **Who do you play with? What are your favourite games?**

16 **Read and number. Then listen and check.**

a Let's play tag! ☐ **b** Let's skip! ☐ **c** Let's play hopscotch! ☐

d Let's play hide and seek! ☐ **e** Let's climb! ☐

17 **Look at 15. Read and match. Then act and say.**

1 1, 2, 3… Where are you? **a** hopscotch

2 Hop, hop, hop! **b** hide and seek

3 Let's run! Run! Run! **c** skipping

4 Jump! Jump! Jump! **d** climbing

5 Up! Up! Up! **e** tag

Jump! Jump! Jump!

PROJECT

18 **Make a Play Time poster. Then present it to the class.**

Play Time

Playtime is fun. I play tag and I jump rope. My favorite game is hopscotch.

content connection (playground games) Unit 9 **157**

²⁴⁷
Look, listen and point. Then say.

1 I like dancing but I don't like skipping. I like dancing with my friends. I like fruit but I don't like salad. My favourite fruit is apples. I also like animals. My favourite animal is a horse.

2 I don't like hopscotch but I like playing tag. I don't like salad but I like pasta. I also don't like frogs but I like snakes and hamsters.

like...	don't like...
I like dancing.	I don't like hopscotch.
I like fruit.	I don't like salad.
I like horses.	I don't like frogs.
He/She/It likes...	He/She/It doesn't like...

I like dancing. I don't like skipping.

20 **Look and write like/don't like.**

1 I _____ kittens.

2 I _____ snakes.

3 I _____ spiders.

4 I _____ turtles.

5 I _____ puppies.

6 I _____ horses.

kittens	✗
snakes	✓
spiders	✓
turtles	✓
puppies	✗
horses	✗

21 **Read and circle.**

1 I **likes** / **like** board games.

2 Toprak **likes** / **like** CDs.

3 Ben **doesn't like** / **don't like** dancing.

4 I **don't like** / **doesn't like** playing tag.

5 Leyla **like** / **likes** computers.

6 Patty **don't like** / **doesn't like** watching TV.

22 **Draw three things you like and three things you don't like. Talk with a partner.**

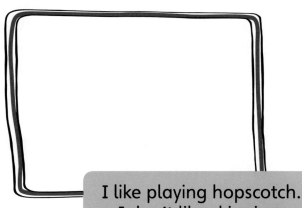

I like playing hopscotch.
I don't like skipping.

grammar (*I like dancing. He doesn't like salad.*) Unit 9 **159**

248

23 Look and listen. Say and do the action.

Rock, Paper, Scissors
Same Game... Different Name!

1

2

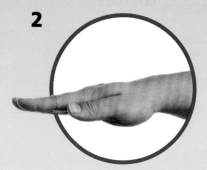

3

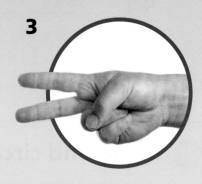

 249

24 Listen and read. Where do they call this game Cachipún

1

Canada

2

Japan

3

Chile

I'm Eva. I'm nine. I play Rock, Paper, Scissors in Canada. I play with my sisters and my best friend, Tina. I always win.

I'm Michio. I'm seven. I'm from Japan. I play this game at school with my friends. We call it Janken. I sometimes win.

I'm Raúl. I'm eight. I'm from Chile. We play this game, too. We call it Cachipún. My brother, Martin, is the best player in our family.

25 Look at 24. Read and ✔.

1 Who always wins?	Tina	☐	Eva	☐
2 Who plays with his friends?	Martin	☐	Michio	☐
3 Who plays with his brother?	Michio	☐	Raúl	☐
4 Who sometimes wins?	Michio	☐	Eva	☐
5 Who is the best player?	Tina	☐	Martin	☐
6 Who plays with her sisters?	Eva	☐	Tina	☐

²⁵⁰
26 Look, listen and say. Play with a friend.

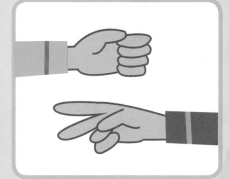 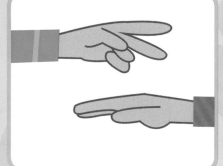 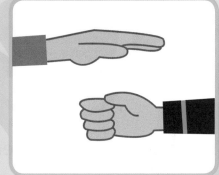

1 Rock breaks scissors. Rock wins!

2 Scissors cut paper. Scissors win!

3 Paper covers rock. Paper wins!

 Do you play Rock, Paper, Scissors in your country? What do you call it? Who do you play with? Who wins?

27 252 Listen and find the picture. Then listen and repeat.

1

2

3

28 253 Listen and number. Then say.

a

Get enough exercise.

b

Get enough sleep.

c

Get enough food and drink.

THINK BIG How do you look after your body?

29 **Listen, look and repeat.**

1 SS   **2** Z   **3** ZZ

 30 **Listen and find. Then say.**

  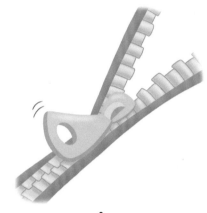

buzz   **kiss**   **zip**

 31 **Listen and blend the sounds.**

1 m-e-ss mess   **2** z-a-p zap   **3** f-i-zz fizz
4 m-i-ss miss   **5** j-a-zz jazz

 32 **Underline ss, z and zz. Then listen and chant.**

Buzz goes the bee.
Zip, zap!
It misses me!

33 Listen and circle.

34 Look at 33. Ask and answer.

Is he skipping?

Yes, he is.

Are they jumping?

No, they aren't.
They're running.

260
 35 **Listen and number.**

a

b

c

d

e

f

36 **Read and match.**

a

b

 I like
I don't like

c

d

I Can

- [ ] **talk about actions and what I like/don't like.**
- [ ] **talk about games children play.**
- [ ] **say how I look after my body.**

Do I Know It?

1 Look and circle. Practise.

☺ I know this. ☹ I don't know this.

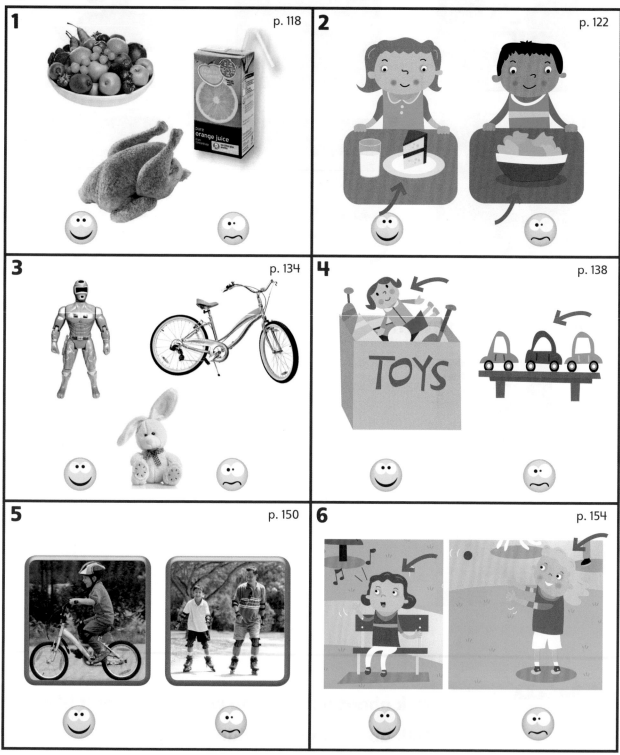

I Can Do It!

262 263

2 Get ready.

A Look. Listen to the questions. Circle the correct words.

1 It's on the **shelf / table**.
2 They're **on / under** the bed.
3 Yes, **he / she** has.

B Listen again and check. Then practise with a partner.

C Look at **A**. Answer these questions with a partner.

  1 What food can you see? What drinks can you see?

  2 How many toys can you see? What are they?

  3 What day is it?

3 **Draw.**

STEP 1 Cut out the outline on page 185.

STEP 2 Fold the paper to make a book.

STEP 3 Write in your book. Colour the front. Now you're ready to **Go!**

4 **Go!**

A Read your book with three classmates. Take turns. Write the presents.

Classmate	Present
Bruno	a train
1	
2	
3	

B Look at your books. Answer these questions with a partner.
1 Page 2: What are they doing?
2 Page 3: What food and drink have they got?
3 Page 3: Where's the cat?
4 Page 4: How many presents can you see?

5 **Draw.**

All About Me

My favourite food is:

My favourite toy is:

Do I Know It Now?

6 **Think about it.**

A Go to page 166. Look and circle again.

B Tick (✔).

☐   I can ask my teacher for help.

☐   I can practise.

7 **Rate this Checkpoint. Colour the stars.**

☆ easy   ☆ hard   ☆ fun   ☆ not fun

1
2
3
4
5
6
7
8
9

Units 7–9 Exam Preparation

– Part A –

 Listen and draw lines. There is one example.

– Part B –

Look and read. Write *yes* or *no*.

Examples

The boy has got ice cream.	*yes*
The ducks are swimming in the sea.	*no*

Questions

1	A girl is riding a red bike.	_____
2	The grandma is reading a book.	_____
3	A girl is catching a ball.	_____
4	A man is drinking milk.	_____
5	A woman is eating crisps.	_____

Young Learners English Practice Starters: Listening A

– 5 questions –

Look at the picture. Now listen and colour. There is one example

Young Learners English Practice Starters: Listening B

– 5 questions –

Look at the pictures. Now listen and draw lines. There is one example.

Young Learners English Practice Starters: Listening C

– 5 questions –

Look at the pictures. Now listen and tick (✔). There is one example.

What's she wearing?

A

B ☐

C ☐

1   Is your brother eating?

A ☐

B ☐

C ☐

2   What's she doing?

A ☐

B ☐

C ☐

3 What are they?

A ☐

B ☐

C ☐

4 What are the cats doing?

A ☐

B ☐

C ☐

5 What are his favourite clothes?

A ☐

B ☐

C ☐

Young Learners English Practice Starters: Reading & Writing A

– 5 questions –

Look and tick. Put a tick (✔) or a (✗) in the box.
There are two examples.

Examples

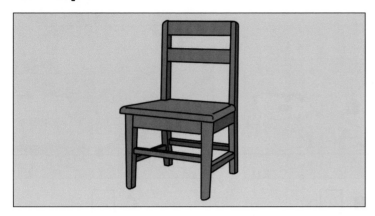

This is a chair. ✔

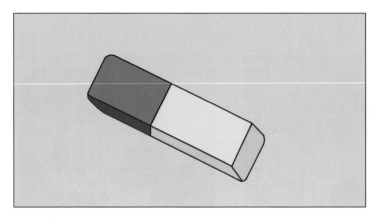

This is a ruler. ✗

Questions

1

This is a baby. ☐

2

This is a foot. ☐

3

This is a book. ☐

4

This is a sister. ☐

5

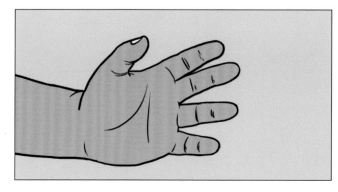

This is a hand. ☐

Young Learners English Practice Starters: Reading & Writing B

– 5 questions –

Look and read. Write *yes* or *no*.

Examples

The farmer is wearing boots.	*yes*
The dog is running.	*no*

Questions

1	The girl is feeding the ducks.	_____
2	The chickens are eating.	_____
3	The girl has got short hair.	_____
4	The boy is reading a book.	_____
5	The farmer has got a red shirt.	_____

Young Learners English Practice Starters: Reading & Writing C

– 5 questions –

Look at the pictures. Look at the letters. Write the words.

Example

t r a i n   a r n t i

Questions

1

_ _ _ _ _ _   g n a o e r

2

_ _ _ _ _ _   t p u p e p

3

_ _ _ _ _   l a d s a

4

_ _ _ _ _ _   t a k s e s

5

_ _ _ _ _ _ _ _   d i n s h c a w

It's My Party!

[name]

I've got a present. It's a
_____. I'm happy today!
[toy]

4

Today is _____ .
[day]

I'm having a party.

2

My friends are eating _____ .
[food]

3

Big English Song

From the mountaintops to the bottom of the sea,
From a big blue whale to a baby bumblebee –
If you're big, if you're small, you can have it all,
And you can be anything you want to be!

It's bigger than you. It's bigger than me.
There's so much to do and there's so much to see!
The world is big and beautiful and so are we!
Think big! Dream big! Big English!

So in every land, from the desert to the sea,
We can all join hands and be one big family.
If we love, if we care, we can go anywhere!
The world belongs to everyone; it's ours to share.

It's bigger than you. It's bigger than me.
There's so much to do and there's so much to see!
The world is big and beautiful and so are we!
Think big! Dream big! Big English!

It's bigger than you. It's bigger than me.
There's so much to do and there's so much to see!
The world is big and beautiful and waiting for me.
A one, two, three...
Think big! Dream big! Big English!

Pearson Education Limited
Edinburgh Gate
Harlow
Essex CM20 2JE
England
and Associated Companies throughout the world.

www.pearsonelt.com/bigenglish

First published 2015
Sixteenth impression 2023

ISBN: 978-1-4479-8908-0

Set in Heinemann Roman
Printed in Slovakia by Neografia

Acknowledgements

The publisher would like to thank the following for their kind permission to reproduce photographs:

(Key: b-bottom; c-centre; l-left; r-right; t-top)

123RF.com: 123RF Limited 160 (Japan), Alexey Astakhov 142 (pizza), andersonrise 128 (Russia), 129/4, Cathy Yeulet 106/25 (Elina), cypher0x 144bl, Darrin Henry 18/19 (4), 25 (d), Dylan Burrill 52 (a), gorgev 106/25 (1), Holger Schmidt 142 (check tablecloth), Hongqi Zhang 106/25 (Sharon), Ivonne Wierink 144br, ka2shka 143/21 (TCL), Karin Lau 90b, Martin Galabov 52 (b), 52 (c), 52 (d), Nat Sukukawadee 106/25 (3), nerthuz 143/21 (TR), Nicolas Nadjar 106/25 (2), pogonici 143/21 (TL), Polsin Janpangpen 106/24 (rabbit), szefei 128 (Korea), 129/3, Tracy Whiteside 106/25 (Zack); **Age Fotostock Spain S.L.:** Ruth Black 104 (d), 108 (playing), Robert Daly 154 (f), Hybrid Images / Cultura 108 (brushing), Image Source 119/5 (4), Insy Shah / Gulf Images 16/15 (3), DU BOISBERRANGER Jean 76 (a), Juice Images 162/27 (2); **Alamy Images:** Aflo Foto Agency 151/1 (a), Anna Maloverjan / Alamy 70/15 (centre right), Caro / Alamy 92/1, Chris Ryan / Alamy 86/15 (4 right), dave stamboulis / Alamy 86/15 (1 left), Friedrich Stark 20/1, imageBROKER 165/36 (d (girl)), IMAGEMORE Co., Ltd. / Alamy 70/15 (centre left), Jeff Morgan 09 156 (skipping), JTB MEDIA CREATION, Inc. 76 (b), Jurgen Magg 156 (hide & seek), Kuttig - People - 2 156 (tag), Semen Lihodeev 64/2, Marco Secchi 74bc, Michael Matthews 86/14 (3), MBI / Alamy 48, 58/6 (left), 130/28 (b), Michael Willis / Alamy 48 (computer), Neil Tingle 74bl, nikreates 118/4, 133/2 (a), 142 (orange juice), 162/28 (c right), 166/1 (TR), ONOKY - Photononstop / Alamy 27t, 32, 58/3, Richard Heyes 143/21 (TCR), RubberBall 20/3, Sally and Richard Greenhill 156 (hopscotch), 158/2 (T), sayoga / Alamy 140/15 (d), Septemberlegs / Alamy 86/15 (2 right), StockImages / Alamy 124/15 (sweet - sugar), Tetra Images / Alamy 41/4 (b), 92/4, 126/2, Wildscape 156 (climbing); **Corbis:** Andersen Ross / Blend Images 54 (a), Heide Benser 80/7, Hero Images 92/2, 124/6, JGI / Jamie Grill, Ocean 26, 30, 35, Vast Photography / First Light / Corbis 54 (b), Wavebreak Media Ltd ; **DK Images:** Andy Crawford 9/17 (point), 18/20 (2), 51 (feet); **Fotolia.com:** air 54 (c), Alexandr Ozerov 70/14 (1), amidala 106/24 (horse), 111/36 (d), Andres Rodriguez 110br, apops 33bl, 33bc, 34/1, 34/3, 79r, Arsgera 89/3, 134/8, Atiketta Sangasaeng 10/1, bARTiko 140/15 (a), byrdyak 88 (d), 96/6, 112/5 (L), 158/1 (B), CandyBox Images 38br, Chris leachman 124/14 (3), dave timms 140/15 (b), Delmas Lehman 111/36 (a), dimedrol68 10/7, 58/2 (pencil), emirkoo 106/24 (dog), 111/36 (c), 126/5, Eric Isselée 57/1 (b), Ever 124/15 (salty - crisps), 125/17 (crisps), fir4ik 48/2, ftfoxfoto 102/14 (4), Gabees 89/1, 95/3, 134/3, 146/4, gemenacom 64/10, 71 (t-shirt), gena96 124/14 (6), 124/15 (salty - chips), 125/17 (fries), Giuseppe Porzani 118/11, 125/17 (pasta), 133/1 (b), Giuseppe_R 41/1 (b), 72/2, 73/3, hellkitty 140/15 (c), heros1973 118/1, 125/17 (cake), 128/23 (L), iofoto 18/19 (5), 151/2 (a), itsallgood 57/4 (a), Iuliia Metkalova 16/15 (2), ivan gusev 140tl, Ivonne Wierink 10/10, jackmicro 86/15 (2 left), 86/15 (4 left), jjpixs 74tc, 150/3, 151tl, 165/35 (b), JM Fotografie, jo 70/14 (2), Joanna Zielinska 150/8, 154 (a), 165/35 (e), 166/5 (L), kilukilu 64/11, 71 (socks), Kimsonal 102/15 (chicken), Konovalov Pavel 64/4, 71 (hat), 112/1 (hat), Kzenon 80/10, 84/1 (b), 95 (a), laszlolorik 16/14 (3), leonidp 96/7, 111/37 (b), 112/5 (c), magann 70/14 (3), Marco Uliana, Maria Mitrofanova 64/7, mdorottya 48 (b), Michael Ireland 150/2, mm3104 57/4 (b), Monkey Business 124/15 (sweet - cookies), 125/17 (cookies), natavin 134/7, 166/3 (B), Natika 124/14 (5), nbiebach 96/1, 106/24 (cat), Nenov Brothers 89/4, 134/5,

135 (a), 149 (f), nerthuz 90c, Noam 41/1 (a), 72/1, 79l, Pavel Losevsky 48/1, PhG 86/15 (1 right), picsfive 48 (ice cream), 124/14 (2), 125/17 (chocolate), Picture-Factory 57/2 (a), pio3 150/6, 151/2 (b), RainLedy 48 (perfume), rakjung2 96/5, 111/37 (d), Roijoy 71bl, RTimages 118/2, 125/17 (fruit), 133/4 (c), 158/1 (T), 166/1 (TL), Rudolf Tepfenhart 70/14 (6), Schlierner 10/6, Sergii Figurnyi 86/15 (3 left), SergiyN 34/4, 41/3 (b), 73/2, simmittorok 10/9, sommersby 64/12, 112/1 (shirt), stockphoto-graf 133/4 (b), sumnersgraphicsinc 124/15 (sweet - chocolate), tan4ikk 130/28 (c), Tatyana Gladskih 16/14 (2), 18/19 (3), Tetiana Zbrodko 95/1, 134/10, 146/1, 149 (d), thawats 51 (hands), The Josh 70/14 (4), thepoo 16/14 (4), Vaida 102/15 (cow), 104 (c), Vasiliy Koval 46b, 57/1 (a), vgm6 102/15 (dog), Viktor 118/9, 118/10, 124/14 (4), 124/15 (salty - salt), 125/17 (chicken), 125/17 (salt), 130/29 (a), 133/1 (c), 133/3 (c), 166/1 (B), Vit 134/1, 166/3 (TL), vlorzor 64/13, 71 (shorts), windu 64/6, 71 (trousers), Wojciech Sobiech 41/3 (a), xalanx 104 (a), 108 (feeding), Yasonya 118/6, 133/2 (c), 133/4 (a), Ziablik 134/11, 149 (c); **Getty Images:** Andrew Bain 70/15 (centre), Anwar Hussein / WireImage 74br, Beto Hacker / The Image Bank 80/5, 84/4 (b), Jon Shireman / The Image Bank 86/14 (1), Paul Bradbury 80/4, 112/3 (TR), Andrea Chu 162/27 (1), Peter Dazeley 81, 84/1 (a), Digital Vision 18/19 (6), 25 (a), 80/12, 84/3 (b), Fuse 80/11, 95 (c), 112/4 (R), Peter Cade / Iconica 80/1, 112/3 (TL), Bruno Morandi / Robert Harding World Imagery 86/14 (2), Susanna Price / Dk Images 80/3, 95 (b), Kraig Scarbinsky / Digital Vision 92/3, Photolibrary / David Page Photography 165/36 (a), Ryan McVay / Stone 84/2 (b), Sophia Vourdoukis / Stone 80/8, 84/3 (a), 112/4 (L), Vstock LLC 95 (d); **Glow Images:** Alex Mares-Manton 154 (b), 165/35 (f), 166/5 (R); **Imagestate Media:** Phovoir 9/18 (b); **Pearson Education:** 5, 43, 46tl, 47t, 49bl, 50 (desk & eraser), 87br, 96/8, 103 (poster), 125bl (poster), 158/2 (poster); **Pearson Education Ltd:** Studio 8 89/2, 95/2, 134/6, 149 (b), Trevor Clifford 6tl, 6tr, 6bl, 6br, 7l, 7r, 8l, 8r, 9/17 (clap), 11l, 11r, 15l, 15r, 18/20 (1), 19 (boy), 19 (girl), 21, 27bl, 27br, 31l, 31r, 33tl, 33tr, 47bl, 47br, 49t, 51bl, 51br, 53l, 53r, 56bl, 56br, 65cl, 65cr, 71cl, 71cr, 74 (girl), 75l, 75r, 76bl, 76br, 85l, 85r, 87tl, 87tr, 89bl, 89br, 91l, 91r, 97bl, 97br, 101l, 101r, 103tl, 103tr, 105l, 105r, 107, 108bl, 108br, 119bl, 119br, 123l, 123r, 125/18 (right), 127l, 127r, 132l, 132r, 135bl, 135br, 139l, 139r, 140tr, 141tl, 141tr, 143bl, 143br, 144cl, 145l, 145r, 148l, 148r, 151bl, 151br, 155l, 155r, 158/1 (girl), 158/2 (boy), 164l, 164r, Rafal Trubisz 144/24 (TL); **Pearson Education Ltd:** Trevor Clifford 9/17 (stand), 9/18 (a), 9/18 (c), 9/18 (d), 18/20 (3), 18/20 (4); **PhotoDisc:** Tony Gable. C Squared Studios 48 (c); **Photolibrary.com:** Image Source 150/5, 158/1 (C); **Shutterstock.com:** 142 (sandwich), 162/28 (c left), AnetaPics 110/2, Anneka 102/14 (2), 104 (b), 111/37 (a), Yuri Arcurs 18/19 (1), 25 (c), 42r, 58/5, Arvind Balaraman 119tl, Gyorgy Barna 80/2, 84/2 (a), 162/27 (3), Chris Bence 118/7, 128/23 (R), 133/3 (a), Ingvar Bjork 10/5, 58/2 (pen), Ruth Black, Mihai Blanaru 74tl, 165/35 (a), BlankaB 106/25 (Flag - Australia), Bragin Alexey 124/14 (1), 125/17 (sugar), Brooke Becker 16/14 (1), charnsitr 106/25 (Flag - USA), chatursunil 57/2 (b), Palle Christensen 125/17 (orange juice), Chros 160/1-3, Condor 36 128 (United States), 129/2, David Pirvu 41/2 (b), 72/3, DenisNata 119/5 (3), Digital Media Pro 48/4, discpicture 40, djgis 96/10, 111/36 (b), Doug Lemke 86/15 (3 right), Jaimie Duplass 150/9, 157t, ffolas 133/1 (a), 142 (salad), Mike Flippo 162/28 (a), Fotogroove 106/25 (Flag - Japan), Gelpi JM 49c, Gemenacom 9/19 (left), 9/19 (right), gengirl 102/15 (cat), Volodymyr Goinyk 70/14 (5), Golden Pixels LLC 108 (walking), Greenland 150/7, 151/1 (b), Happy person 48 (a), 65b, Margo Harrison 134/2, 135 (c), 146/3, haveseen 80/6, 112/3 (B), 126/3, Darrin Henry 17, 41/2 (a), 73/1, Horiyan 118/5, 130/29 (b), Mau Horng 124/15 (sweet - cake), 133/3 (b), iofoto 106/25 (Reiko), Eric Isselee 95/4, 97tl (goat), 97tr (goat), 110/4, Jacek Chabraszewski 165/36 (c), Jenkedco 128 (Mexico), 129/2, Karkas 64/5, 64/8, Katstudio 124/15 (salty - pizza), Joana Kruse 119/5 (1), Lucie Lang 10/3, 50 (crayon), 58/1 (crayon), Aliaksei Lasevich 70/15 (bottom), 74tr, Lenkadan 97 (a), 110/1, Leroy Harvey 142 (burger), Alexander Mak 88 (a), 102/14 (3), mamahoohooba 141b, Martin Nemec 88 (c), 96/3, 97 (b), 112/5 (R), mathom 88 (b), 102/14 (1), Vladimir Melnikov 154 (e), michaeljung 18/19 (2), 25 (b), 41b (c), 65tr, Stuart Monk 86/14 (4), Monkey Business Images 34/2, 41b (a), 58/4, 103br, 119/5 (2), Pavel V Mukhin 64/1, 71 (boots), 112/1 (boots), Amy Myers 150/4, 165/35 (d), Lisovskaya Natalia 10/2, Nattika 165/36 (d cheese), Nenov Brothers Images 144/24 (TCL), Nikonboy 90tr, Michal Ninger 97 (c), 110/3, nito 144/24 (TCR), nrt 118/8, 130/29 (d), 158/2 (C), Olga Syzranova 80/9, 84/4 (a), 95 (e), 126/1, 162/28 (b), Alon Othnay 154 (c), M. Unal Ozmen 125/17 (ice cream), panco971 165/36 (b), PhotoNAN 64/9, Olga Popova, ppfoto13 64/3, Alexander Raths 46tr, 58/6 (right), 119tr, Randy Rimland 96/4, Karen Roach 10/8, 118/3, 128/23 (C), 133/2 (b), Rob Marmion 20/2, Anatoliy Samara 165/15 (1), 157b, Sean Locke Photography 160 (Chile), Anna Sedneva 95/4 (oats), 97t (oats), 110/4 (oats), SergiyN 69r, 112/2 (R), Valery Shklovskiy 96/2, Roman Sigaev, Sofarina79 154 (d), Stephanie Frey 144cr, Margaret M Stewart 10/4, Kuttelvaserova Stuchelova 33br, swissmacky 57/3 (b), Tatik22 134/9, 149 (a), Tony Taylor 111/37 (c), Leah-Anne Thompson 150/1, 165/35 (c), juan carlos tinjaca 49br, V_Krv 48 (MP3), V. J. Matthew 90tl, Val Thoermer 130/28 (a), Valentina_S 96/9, viki2win 160 (Canada), VojtechVlk 41/4 (a), Tatyana Vychegzhanina 151tr, wacpan 134/4, 135 (b), 144/24 (TR), 146/2, 149 (e), 166/3 (TR), YanLev 41b (b), 73/4, Kisialiou Yury 48 (d), ZouZou 165/36 (d boy)); **Sozaijiten:** 106/25 (4); **SuperStock:** 48/3, age fotostock 38bl, Blend Images